BUILD RESILIENCE

BUILD RESILIENCE

Live, Learn, and Lead

Lucy Chen

MANUSCRIPTS
PRESS

BUILD RESILIENCE
Live, Learn, and Lead

ISBN
979-8-88926-538-2   *Paperback*
979-8-88926-539-9   *Ebook*

To my father, who nurtured me.

CONTENTS

INTRODUCTION

———

"Where is BaoBao?" my mom asked, eagerly scanning the rows in front of us.

BaoBao is my eldest daughter's nickname. We were attending her college graduation ceremony at Yankee Stadium on May 18, 2022. There was a celebratory atmosphere on that fresh, crisp morning. By 10:30 a.m., the stadium was full of family members attending the NYU commencement. I pointed toward the seating area where the students sat. "She must be over there." Mom's eyes sparkled with excitement as she looked for BaoBao. But at that moment, my mind wandered to my father, and tears welled up uncontrollably. How I wished he could be there to share that memorable moment with us.

Dad had passed away five months earlier. Because one of his fondest wishes was to celebrate my eldest daughter's college graduation, I felt heartache since he did not live long enough to see that day. My parents went to college in China and graduated in the early 1960s. Like most Chinese parents, they emphasized education and attended my graduation from

UCLA in 1996. It was one of their happiest days. I realized how much Dad treasured that moment after finding my graduation picture on his bed stand when sorting through his important documents after his passing. He obviously cherished it since his dream of raising me and providing the best education came true that day. Twenty-six years later, I can also proudly say my dream of raising my daughter and giving her the best education possible came true as well.

Compared to my parents, my children are incredibly fortunate to have avoided the hardships of extreme poverty and starvation experienced during WWII, the Chinese Civil War, and the Great Chinese Famine. Life was tough for everyone in China from the 1930s through the '60s. China was one of the world's poorest countries since only ten countries had a lower per capita GDP than China (Prashad and Ross 2021). Statista reported the high infant mortality rate in China in 1950 when nearly one in five did not survive past their first birthday (O'Neill 2022), compared to 2.92 percent in the United States in 1950 (IOM 2003).

My children also did not have to face the food shortage experienced by my peers and me when we relied on food rationing cards issued by the Chinese government, which they sorted by age and gender. They did not experience my struggle when immigrating to a new country with culture and language barriers. Instead, they enjoy abundant resources, comfortable living conditions, nutritious food, education, and career options. If someone had predicted our current living conditions when I was little, I would have dismissed it as fiction. But that's what older generations, including mine, dreamed about and strived for.

I thought about my parents, who endured numerous hardships from WWII to the Cultural Revolution. During their lifetime, one-sixth of China's population became in-country refugees (Klein 2022), and nearly thirty million died during the Great Leap Forward between 1960 and 1962 (Brown 2012).

"What helped you survive those tough times?" I asked Dad.

"We had no choice," he replied.

I asked Mom, "What pushed you forward to become successful in life?"

"Optimism. Never give up." She smiled at me. "I'm lucky," she added.

Being optimistic definitely helped her and kept her dreaming of a bright future during dark moments. Resilience is another trait she and Dad shared. Since living through difficult times can take a heavy toll on one's mood and health, my parents often felt helpless and overwhelmed by stress and anxiety. Nonetheless, they overcame those challenges. Based on their stories, I discovered several characteristics behind their success—resilience, optimism, initiative, kindness, hope, commitment, dedication, and more. These traits helped them thrive in a tough world.

As I reflect on the journey of three generations in my family—my parents, myself, and now my children—I contemplate whether my children and their peers truly appreciate the resources they have and whether they possess the grit needed to face the storms that life may bring. How can today's young people learn from the wisdom and experiences of previous generations, ensuring they carry forward the values of gratitude, adaptability, and strength?

Throughout my diverse careers in engineering, consulting, risk management, and renewable energy, I've taken on the role of a mentor and coach, especially for immigrants, women, and young Americans. Understanding their struggles and those of young people today, I firmly believe in their capacity to heal and grow. Everyone can learn lessons about resilience from those who have experienced life's hardships before tapping into their innate strengths to live a more successful life. To build resilience, we need to start with nurturing and healing our body and mind, changing the narratives in our minds, and gaining power through our experience and support system. What does not kill us makes us strong.

As of now, our lives have almost gone back to where they were before the COVID-19 pandemic, even though some areas in the US still require masks while other places in the world remain in high alert mode. However, life also seems to have become more stressful than ever before. An overwhelming majority of people in the United States think the country is experiencing a mental health crisis (McPhillips 2022).

What are the reasons behind the stress? Psychologist Mary Karapetian Alvord claims uncertainty is the biggest stressor for her US clients. The 2022 Deloitte Gen Z and Millennial Survey corroborates her findings, stating that stress and anxiety remain at heightened levels for both generations, most notably in younger respondents (Global Talent 2022).

In a world of uncertainty, we need to build resilience to manage stress and face setbacks and daily challenges. Resilience is the process and outcome of successfully adapting to difficulties and tragedies, especially through behavioral flexibility and adjustment to external and internal demands (*American Psychological Association* 2022). Each one of us will inevitably encounter life's challenges. How we respond to them determines our success.

I wrote this book to benefit people who feel stuck in life. It's also for people who worry about the future, given the uncertainty of the world, as well as for those who are arriving in this country, feeling insecure or inadequate. I'd like to let readers know they can face all challenges and bounce back from any situation. In short, this book is for anyone who would like to develop resilience and live an abundant life.

In Part I of the book, I share many stories of my family, spanning over eighty years and across two countries: China and the US. In Part II, I draw from these personal stories to develop seven principles of building resilience.

1. Nurturing and healing
2. Goals, hopes, and dreams
3. Gratefulness and contentment
4. Spirituality and faith
5. Growth
6. Community and connection
7. A simple life

Even in this era of the internet and advanced technology, the skills of older generations can help people thrive by changing fixed mindsets, beliefs, and habits. Believe in your own strength and use it to build a bright future.

Human beings are resilient. We have the innate strength and power to survive and thrive in this ever-evolving world. We can learn, grow, and improve in the face of challenges, and we are stronger than we thought across generations. Resilience can build and improve through nurturing the body and soul, maintaining hopes and goals, practicing gratitude, relying on faith, continuing improvement, and connecting with others. Let us journey to my parents' generation and see what they went through and how they survived.

PART I

LIFE STORIES

CHAPTER 1

MY FATHER'S STORY

CHILDHOOD

My father, Dabao, was born in Beijing in 1936. The Chinese characters of his name spell out *big protection*, embodying strength and courage.

The next year, Japan invaded China on a full scale and started the eight-year-long bloody war as part of WWII. According to some historians, World War II actually began outside of Beijing on July 7, 1937—rather than in Poland or Pearl Harbor. On that day, Japanese and Chinese troops clashed, and within a few days, the local conflict had transformed into a full, though undeclared, war between China and Japan (Mitter 2023). Back then, Nanjing (or Nanking) was the capital of China. In December 1937, over a period of six weeks, the Imperial Japanese Army forces brutally murdered hundreds of thousands of people. The deaths included both soldiers and civilians. They killed an estimated range from 200,000 to 300,000 people.

In many areas, Japan carried out the "three-alls policy," a campaign of "Kill all, burn all, loot all." The Japanese slaughtered villagers throughout China, stole their food, and burned their homes to the ground. By 1942, the Japanese army occupied the northern cities of China, including Beijing. *Pacific Atrocities Education* reported, "Japan had possession of roughly 25 percent of China's enormous territory and more than a third of its entire population. Beyond its areas of direct control, Japan carried out bombing campaigns, looting, massacres, and raids deep into Chinese territory. Almost no place was beyond the reach of Japanese intrusion" (Witzke 2017).

The attacks devastated the entire country as people lived in fear and panic. The Japanese army seized Beijing, Dabao's hometown, in 1937. At the beginning of the war, Dabao's family enjoyed a modest lifestyle—not rich, but not destitute either. However, the war brought misery and anxiety to everyone.

For a period of time, civilians hid from the Japanese soldiers. Dabao's family was no different. Whenever someone in the neighborhood signaled that the Japanese were coming, everyone would quickly withdraw and hide under any building structure they could find.

One fateful day, everyone in the neighborhood ran into a nearby tunnel after hearing that the Japanese were coming. While everyone was quietly holding their breath, Dabao, then an infant, began crying. No matter how much his mother tried to comfort him, he persisted.

Everyone was nervous and yelled at his family. "Whose baby is still crying? If the Japanese find us, they will kill everyone."

Amid the chaos, someone shouted at him to be quiet, but it only made things worse. He got more scared and cried even louder. "Please, please, my baby!" Dabao's mom pleaded with him. She tried everything to soothe him—rocking, cuddling, and hushing, but he would not stop crying. Someone started yelling at his mother to abandon the baby. She refused initially but caved in under immense pressure. She tearfully put down Dabao at the entrance of the tunnel, hoping to leave him there so he might stop crying. It was an agonizing choice, for he was her beloved son, and the thought of leaving him behind broke her heart. But keeping him could endanger everyone else. Frightened, she wept.

Dabao's grandmother's expression turned stern and resolute in that harrowing moment. As rage boiled within her, she went against the cries of others and scooped him up, refusing to abandon him to his fate.

"No. I am not going to leave you here by yourself. Grandma is here with you," she whispered, gently massaging his head.

She, a tiny woman with bound feet, held her beloved grandson close and walked out of that tunnel firmly without looking back. Deciding to stay with him till the last minute, she prepared for the worst: if he died, she would die with him. Fortunately, the Japanese army did not find anyone nearby, sparing them from the horror that could have happened. The day that could have been a tragedy transformed into a tale of courage, resilience, and love. Dad's family told the legendary story many times. That was the first time he almost lost his life.

Just like many ordinary families, his family fell into poverty due to the scarcity of resources and reduced income caused by the war. By 1945, China had fought for eight years, longer than any other Allied power. It lost perhaps fourteen million people, second only to the Soviet Union (Wingfield-Hayes 2015). In August of that year, Japan surrendered to the Allied forces, thereby ending WWII.

However, the war's end did not mark the end of conflict in China. The Chinese Civil War soon followed on its heels as it was a fight between the Nationalists and the Communists (The Editors of *Encyclopaedia Britannica*, 2023). The civil war added more suffering to those struggling to survive the Japanese invasion. *The Collector* reported that the Chinese Civil War was the bloodiest in modern history, given the massive atrocities and massacres that led to civilian casualties of between 1.8 and 3.5 million. He ranks it as the third bloodiest war of the twentieth century after the two world wars (Benabdeljalil 2023).

Dabao's family became even more impoverished during the wars that lasted for more than a decade. His father was the only one who worked even though his salary was far from sufficient to support his mother, wife, and three children. Dabao learned from a tender age the importance of helping out around the house. As the eldest son in the family, he felt it was his duty to provide for his loved ones. His grandmother, who had saved his life during the war, held him dear and constantly affirmed, "You are my eldest grandson. You are awesome."

Driven by this affection and responsibility, Dabao started to search for possible jobs, and the most suitable one was selling newspapers. Even though he was only six years old, he forced himself to get up before 5 a.m. to get to the newspaper distribution center with other children of approximately his age. If he showed up late, he could not sell newspapers in his neighborhood because others would have already covered the area. He learned to get up early each morning and run fast to beat other kids. He would spend the whole morning yelling and selling his newspapers. He had to bear the loss for any newspapers unsold by the end of the day.

Dark and cold winters were the worst. With an empty stomach, Dabao often dragged his feet to sell the last newspaper. One day, he was too exhausted to move because he had perspired too much from hunger. As he sat down to rest after a full morning of selling newspapers, he passed out for a few minutes. The howling wind and freezing pavement woke him, but he was too weak to move.

Then, he realized he was close to his uncle's house, so he slowly walked in, greeting them, "Uncle, Aunt, good morning!"

Although he was too embarrassed to ask for food, his uncle seemed to know Dabao was hungry. He invited Dabao in with a warm smile, "Good timing, we just prepared noodles for lunch; come join us," before handing him a pair of chopsticks.

Dabao nodded and quietly sat down by the table. He inhaled the food swiftly. He told me it was the best food he had ever had in his life. Since there were some green beans in the noodles, he began to consider green bean noodles the best dish ever. Needless to say, he appreciated his uncle giving him a good meal that day.

One summer, he had a mosquito bite on his right leg when he was about ten years old. He did not pay attention to it until the bite area started oozing yellowish pus and became painful. (He probably scratched the area, so the skin got infected.) But as a young boy, he did not want to trouble his mother and grandmother, so the pain worsened over the next two months. The infected areas spread, swelling up, as more pus oozed out. When it became too painful for him to walk, his mother and grandmother tried different methods to treat it, but to no avail. Even the local experienced doctor in the neighborhood ran out of ideas. He worried Dabao would lose his leg if things got worse. Fortunately, the wound was in his calf area rather than the front side, where the infection could easily have entered the bone.

Time passed quickly. Then winter arrived, and the infected area expanded, growing even more painful. One day, he went to the nearby church to pick up some free food. At that time, with war and chaos, the nearby church set up a food distribution center for the poor.

Dabao casually mentioned his wound to the priest and asked, "Sir, do you have any medicine to treat it?"

The priest with gray hair was a foreigner who was very kind to little children. He searched all his meager belongings and found toothpaste powder. He handed it to Dabao, saying, "Son, give it a try. It has an anti-infection ingredient, so it might be useful."

Even though he was not sure it could heal Dabao's wound, it was the best medicine he could find. Grateful for the priest's blessing, Dabao thanked him and dashed back home. He believed in this kind old man, thinking that medicine must have magic power. He put the toothpaste powder on his wound twice a day. After one week, his wound dried. A week later, the infected area began to shrink, and it completely healed after two to three weeks. It felt like a miracle after three to four months of intense suffering. With his leg saved by the magic powder, Dabao was grateful for the priest's help and learned to take good care of himself.

The Chinese Civil War finally ended on October 1, 1949, when Mao Zedong, the leader of the Communists, proclaimed the establishment of the People's Republic of China in Beijing. By the end of the same year, virtually all of mainland China was under communist control. That marked the end of the civil war, which lasted for four years. People finally welcomed a peaceful life.

However, Dabao's father became ill and eventually passed away not long after. The family felt desolate with the weaker and older members—Dabao's grandmother, his mom, his older sister, his little brother, who was about six years old, and himself. The burden of supporting the family fell on the shoulders of the two widows, Dabao's grandmother and mother. Both were traditional women with limited education, skills, and work experience. When his father fell sick, both women had to find various ways to support the family—sometimes babysitting other children or washing and mending clothes for others—on top of working around the house. At just fourteen years old, Dabao felt it was his duty to support the whole family because he had suddenly become the man of the house.

Dabao and his sister had to find more jobs to make ends meet. One of the jobs they took was working as laborers in a bicycle factory where the work was strenuous, the hours long, and the income meager. Exhausted from carrying heavy metals and tires all day, all they wanted to do after work was to lie down and sleep. The demanding physical labor left them drained, and rest was their only respite from the toils of the day.

There was not enough food, so everyone in the family sometimes only had one meal a day. Although Dabao's stomach was constantly growling, he never wanted to complain about it. His pet dog, Huazi, spent most days sniffing the trash on the street because the family could not feed him much. Sometimes, he was lucky enough to find some leftover food at the corner of the street to fill his empty stomach. One day, Dabao's mother brought home money; it probably was her payday. She then bought corn flour and made some steamed buns. Before she called everyone to come and enjoy the buns, Huazi dashed to the table excitedly, barking loudly, jumping up and down, and wagging his tail joyfully. He could not wait and licked one delicious bun he had not tasted for several weeks. He dropped the bun to the ground and was about to eat it.

Dabao's mother got mad and yelled at him. "Bad dog! How dare you! Children have not had any!"

Huazi paused and grunted a little. He put his head down and picked up the bun, carrying it to Grandmother's foot. He must have felt ashamed.

Dabao showed up and saw the whole thing. He begged his mother, "Mom, he's so pitiful… Can he eat some of mine?"

His mother sighed as she also took pity on Huazi.

"No need to let him eat your share. Just eat yours," she told Dabao.

Then she ordered Huazi, "Fine, take this bun and eat it."

Huazi did not dare to eat it this time, so he stared at Grandmother and Dabao carefully. Grandmother softened her tone to allow him to eat.

Dabao also patted his head. "There, there, go ahead to eat. You are a good boy."

Then, Huazi munched on his bun quickly and happily.

Throughout Dabao's childhood, he battled hunger, illness, the loss of his father, and unrelenting labor. However, he nurtured a flame of hope for a brighter tomorrow. His heart swelled with gratitude for the warmth of his family's embrace. He shared a special bond with his grandmother, a woman of resilience and strength who weathered her own storms, including raising four children but tragically losing three. Her optimism became a beacon, lighting the path for Dabao and the entire family to follow.

ADULTHOOD
Despite working to support his family, Dabao continued to attend school. His father, a knowledgeable man, instilled in him the importance of diligent study and learning. He cherished the opportunity for education, which was not widely available for the poor—especially girls like his older sister. He felt fortunate.

At the end of the Chinese Civil War in 1949, very few attended schools or even had basic literacy skills. The Communist Party implemented policies to improve access to education for all and reduce the illiteracy rate. *The New York Times* reports that amid the national economic recovery (1949–1952), the government prioritized ensuring basic education rights for the impoverished, supporting new schools, and bolstering primary education. Moreover, in the initial stages of communism, the government embraced Soviet education models, with a strong emphasis on engineering and production labor, to rapidly reshape the education system (TAO, BERCI, and WAYNE 2023).

Dabao and his siblings benefited from the education system after the founding of New China in 1949. Like many children, they never stopped working on the side. Dabao entered the workforce after high school. His earnings improved the family's living conditions, allowing him to support his grandmother, mother, and younger brother. His older sister also found a better and more stable job, got married, and moved out. As the bread earner for the family, he was happy and proud of his contribution to his loved ones.

In 1958, the government launched the Great Leap Forward to transform the country from an agrarian economy into a communist society. China needed more talent in the area of science and technology. In the same year, the Chinese Academy of Sciences in Beijing founded the University of Science and Technology of China (USTC) with the goal of cultivating the country's most promising scientific and technological talent (*The Times Higher Education* 2023).

Years of war left the country in ruins, with much restoration needed. With the high demand for talent in science and technology, the Chinese government covered all tuition and living expenses for all college students across the country in the 1950s and '60s while providing students from low-income families with monthly subsidies. These new benefits proved beneficial, especially for the most impoverished.

Dabao eagerly grasped the opportunity and applied to the university. With his outstanding academic achievements, the University of Science and Technology of China accepted him, where he majored in solid physics and became one of the first batch of graduates of the university in four years. At twenty-one that year, he was not only very bright and academically strong but also had hands-on experience with engineering design. Cherishing the opportunity to study at one of the most prestigious Chinese colleges, he studied hard and immersed himself in knowledge. But he managed to enjoy himself too. His college drafted him to play basketball because of his tall physique and athletic skills.

Little did he sense that another storm was brewing. Between the spring of 1959 and the end of 1961, China experienced what was arguably the world's largest famine, during which some thirty million people starved to death and about the same number of births lost or postponed (Smil 1999). The rationed food quota was far from enough for everyone, especially for adult men who needed more calories in daily activities. Many people often fainted from hunger, while malnutrition was common.

Dabao moved to his college campus at the beginning of the school year, which also happened to lighten the burden on his family. Staying away from home prevented his mother and grandmother from sharing their already scarce food with him. It was common practice for women to distribute a larger portion of food to the men in the family since women generally consumed less than their allotted quota. On campus, he relied solely on his own food quota, which insufficient for his tall frame, especially as an active sportsman.

One afternoon, Dabao went to practice basketball as part of his daily routine. He felt exhausted after less than half an hour, and his clothes were quickly drenched with sweat. Deciding to rest, he was about to sit down on the ground to catch his breath. Suddenly, he felt dizzy, and his legs wobbled. Clinging to the wall, he slowly lowered himself to the ground and lost consciousness.

Loud noises and the coldness of the air woke him. Feeling exhausted, hungry, and thirsty, he stood up and slowly walked toward his dorm. Fainting was common in those days. Everyone knew it boiled down to a lack of food, for which the common solution was to drink water to fill the stomach. Returning to his dorm, Dad ran into a friend in the hallway.

"Have you heard doctors hospitalized a student? This time, it wasn't because of hunger but because of tuberculosis. The doctor said he needs nutrition to recover. His food coupons are not enough," his friend said.

"I can donate my coupons to him. I still have some left for this month," Dabao anxiously said.

"Are you sure? You are tall and need a lot yourself," Dabao's friend reminded him, especially since he had just recovered from fainting. It was obvious that Dabao's food coupons were far from enough.

"Yes, I can tighten my belt more. I will drink more water." Dabao nodded firmly.

He donated his own food coupons for this sick student along with other students. Donating food coupons was tantamount to starving yourself and could even cost you your life. But Dabao felt it was important to save lives. He skipped more meals to save coupons. He felt lucky enough to be healthy and continued to donate his food coupons for several months until doctors discharged that student from the hospital in good health. What sets Dabao apart is his remarkable act of persistently donating his coupons for months to the classmate who was unwell. Such selflessness was uncommon among male students, and it's worth noting Dabao was not only one of the tallest in his college but also needed more nourishment due to his physical activity.

For the following two years or so, he continued to tighten his belt while drinking more water to last through the days of hunger. He also slept more to restore his energy. Although hunger exhausted him, it did not prevent him from studying hard and graduating from college with top scores in 1963. By then, the food shortage situation had improved throughout the country.

Years later, because of his successful career, Dabao received invitations from several organizations to give speeches and receive awards. He donated the earnings to Project Hope, a nonprofit organization in China that aims to build schools in rural, poverty-stricken areas of China to help children whose families cannot afford to complete elementary school. Because he experienced starvation and poverty when he was young, he felt connected to those children, understanding the importance of education and opportunities he felt fortunate enough to enjoy.

MARRIAGE

After graduating from the USTC, Dabao started working as an engineer and physicist at a leading research institute specializing in metal research. Back then, steel production was one of the top priorities for speeding up industrialization, so the institute became one of China's most important research organizations. Dabao worked hard to contribute to these research projects.

By 1964, Dabao had become a competent engineer and researcher in the physics department. One day, his supervisor assigned him a new task: welcoming the newly assigned college graduates to the department. As Dabao opened the door and walked into the room where they were waiting, a female graduate nervously rose from her chair. She thought Dabao was the boss, so she took a deep bow and said, "Greetings!"

Dabao gently smiled at her. "Hello! Welcome to our department. Please sit down."

Seeing such a beautiful and genuine girl with big eyes and long black braids delighted him. After everyone introduced themselves, the girl realized Dabao was not the boss, so she felt embarrassed by her greetings and grew anxious. This girl was my mother, Xiaoqin.

Dabao warmly welcomed everyone by showing them around the department and introducing them to the staff. Xiaoqin felt relaxed afterward. She noticed he was young, tall, and handsome, as well as a gentle, kind, and knowledgeable intellectual.

Dabao specialized in solid-state physics, while Xiaoqin focused on metallurgy physics. Their paths crossed, and they fell in love, becoming engaged in 1965. Years later, they would share a playful laugh about Xiaoqin bowing to him deeply when they met—love at first sight!

A twist of fate emerged by the time they were ready to marry. Dabao received a work assignment that took him to a distant town in Guizhou Province, renowned for its mercury mines. He worked there with his colleagues for several months, which inadvertently delayed their wedding. When Dabao returned to Beijing after the assignment, he felt exhausted and plagued by persistent illness. After visiting doctors and conducting research, he discovered he must have mercury poisoning, given the working conditions and poor personal equipment. He was not alone. Other people seemed to have similar symptoms—fatigue, sleepiness, headache, etc.

When Xiaoqin eagerly discussed their wedding plan, Dabao hesitated.

In a soft tone, Dabao confided, "I'm battling illness now. I may never fully recover. You don't want to marry a sick man. Perhaps you should find a healthier husband."

Xiaoqin got angry but insisted on marrying him. As an orphan, she lacked love and finally found someone very caring and loving. She would not let him go.

Without hesitation, she firmly replied to Dabao. "You will recover. I'm going to take care of you, whether in sickness or in health."

With her determination, they got married in January 1966. Every time I heard this story, shivers would run down my spine, knowing I would not have otherwise been born.

Mom was right as Dad's symptoms finally faded away. As promised, she devoted herself to caring for him throughout their over fifty-year journey together, even through his final bedridden days. Dad's love for Mom was from the bottom of his heart, and he treated her with affection, respect, and reliance. He often reminded us that she was orphaned as a child, enduring numerous hardships, and we should take good care of her. I don't think I've ever seen my parents fight. They always seemed deeply in love with each other. I witnessed with my own eyes what it means to "hold your hand, be by your side till old age." ("执子之手, 与子偕老" originally appeared in The Classic of Poetry (or Shijing), the oldest Chinese poetry dating from the eleventh to seventh centuries BCE. It's a well-known Chinese proverb and idiom that has been passed down through generations and represents enduring love and companionship.)

Soon after their marriage, Xiaoqin became pregnant. The whole family was excited about the new baby. Dabao's eighty-six-year-old grandmother was the happiest family member.

Even though she could barely get up from her bed due to her sickness, she started making cotton jackets and trousers for the baby, who was due in January.

"I am going to make the best baby clothes for my great-grandson!" She told everyone around her.

"Take your time. Still, plenty of time." Dabao's mother comforted his grandmother.

"What if the little one arrives early? Clothes made by a great-grandmother bear blessings. I need to hurry." She probably sensed her days were coming to a close. Dabao's grandmother finished making the baby clothes by the end of December. She was satisfied.

Every morning, Dabao would gently touch his grandmother's hand and bid her farewell as he set off for work, saying, "Goodbye, granny. I'm going to work. See you later." His grandmother would remind him to take good care of himself. Every evening, Dabao would walk to his grandmother's room, his voice softly calling out, "Granny, I'm back." Her face would light up with a smile, embracing his presence with joy. This simple exchange became their cherished daily ritual, a testament to their special bond.

One day in early January, Dabao felt uneasy at work somehow. The unsettling feeling lingered until he received the news in the afternoon. His grandmother had peacefully passed away in her sleep. Dabao believed there was a telepathic bond between family members. When a person died or was in pain, loved ones could feel it even from afar. When he hurried home, he entered his grandmother's room to discover it was empty. Beside her pillow lay the neatly folded baby's clothes, a poignant reminder of her labor of love. Tears welled in his eyes as he realized his comforting words, "Granny, I'm back," were no longer necessary. He grieved for a long time. Without his grandmother, he might have perished during the war. She, his cherished grandmother and closest friend, had always held him close to her heart.

TB

Three years later, I was born in 1970. The entire family was joyful, and Dad proudly announced to everyone, "I have a baby girl now." With excitement, Dad said softly, "Our precious baby girl arrived early in the morning, so let's name her *First Ray of Sunshine*." Mom's smile beamed as she held me close to her heart, nodding in agreement. That's the origin of my Chinese name—carrying boundless joy and hope to our family. Since that day, my parents have long treated me as their radiant sunshine.

Everyone said I looked exactly like Dad, making him extremely happy. Every day, the most rewarding moments for Dad were coming back home from work and gently cradling me in his arms. He had no time to rest, but his heart was full of joy and contentment. Little did he know another unforeseen storm was on the horizon, ready to test his resilience once again.

One day, his deep, persistent coughs alarmed him, so he saw his doctor. The following week, the doctor tentatively diagnosed him with TB (tuberculosis). He was in shock, but it was not completely surprising since he had been coughing for a while, even though other tuberculosis symptoms were absent.

Upon returning home, Dad revealed the devastating news to Mom. "I might have TB."

"Are you sure? What did the doctor say?" Mom's eyes widened with deep concern.

"The doctor was not 100 percent sure. My symptoms were somewhat different. My lung shadow was preexisting," Dad gravely responded. "I used to work in highly polluted areas for research. Remember the mercury mine? I might have had underlying conditions. So, the doctor warned me I might have TB while also suspecting it's from a preexisting lung condition."

"How can we treat it?" Mom's voice held a note of apprehension.

"We can't. There's no conventional treatment," Dad replied with a wry smile. "Also, I need to move out immediately because I have to quarantine. I am moving out now." He began collecting his clothes.

"Don't worry about me. I will recover. Believe me. I don't believe a cure doesn't exist for the disease. I will come and visit you once in a while. You take care!" Dad affectionately looked at Mom.

To err on the side of caution, in case Dad did indeed have TB bacteria, he decided to follow his doctor's advice and undergo a three-month quarantine. Quarantine entailed relocating from our apartment and living separately from us. It did not, however, mean he would vanish from our lives entirely. He still wanted to make weekly visits to assist Mom and spend time with me, but this required him to take extra precautions, such as wearing protective clothing, to prevent any potential germ transmission to his loved ones.

Dad was not afraid because he was young and strong. He had always been cautious of contagious diseases by avoiding large crowds, wearing masks during the winter, washing his hands diligently, and taking other hygienic measures. He trained my brother and me to do the same when we were little. For the most part, he did not believe he had TB, especially since the doctor was not certain, and coughing and lung shadows were the only symptoms.

Dad was an optimistic man. He believed TB was still curable and trusted his body to have a self-healing power. Medical treatment didn't exist, but he believed he could nurture his body. All was not hopeless.

We were poor, but everyone was poor back then. Meat, along with rice and flour, were all rationed. Eggs were the only source of nutrients, but they were hard to find. While pregnant with me, my mother needed nutritious food, which was difficult to get. So, Dad contemplated various ways to procure more.

He finally arrived at an idea. He spoke with the staff who worked in the dining hall of his working unit, persuading them to sell him pork bones at a very cheap price. Everyone considered pork bones precious because you could boil them to make a delicious soup. Since there was no place to buy the bones, a ration card wasn't necessary, and they were free to the people working in the dining hall.

Once or twice a week, Dad would buy those bones and make tomato soup with them. Sometimes, when the dining hall ran out of bones, he would buy them at a butcher's house. Very polite and friendly, he could make friends with anyone on the street. He possessed a sunny disposition and an endearing aura of authenticity, making others more than willing to assist him. Mindful of his condition, he wore a mask and was careful about keeping his distance when chatting to others.

The hardest part was visiting home. Because of his condition, he wanted to self-quarantine for three months, which was very challenging. He longed to hug and kiss me and help Mom care for me. Because our apartment unit was so tiny, about one hundred square feet, he could not quarantine himself away from us. His only choice was to live elsewhere—namely, his office. He brought a single blanket with him and rested on two desks since there was no bed. But he did not feel too uncomfortable.

Fortunately, the days warmed up as summer arrived. He came home once a week to visit us, wearing many layers of masks and gloves to avoid transmitting germs. Despite the heat, he also forced himself to wear multiple layers of clothes despite sweating profusely. Rocking me and watching me smile and giggle, his heart filled with joy and peace.

Dad felt much better three months later, so he visited the doctor again. The doctor ordered x-rays and examined his body, finding that the lung shadow had disappeared completely. Both Dad and his doctor were astonished by the miraculous change. The joyous news filled him with happiness—the end of his three-month office quarantine and a heartwarming homecoming celebration. For years, he attributed the miracle to his optimism and nurturing. It was a story he would relate to me over and over again.

HARDWORKING

In the 1970s, Dabao and his colleagues went to a remote village to work in a cadre school as part of the reeducation policy for intellectuals called for by Mao. While working there, Dabao faced tough times due to the hard labor involved. But he was a quick adapter and embraced the challenging environment. He took pride in carrying more weight than anyone else using a shoulder pole. During the night, many people would play cards and laugh after a day of gruesome farm work, whereas Dabao would use his free time to read and learn English.

One day, his group leader asked him, "Are you using work hours to learn English?"

Dabao shook his head. "No, I have been using my own time." At that time, communist theory was the focus of political study for everyone, especially for the intellectuals in the reeducation camp. They considered the study of English imperialist and capitalist—to the point of considering it a serious crime if any such activity was conducted during working hours.

Dabao thought about it and said, "I work as hard as anyone else... I am willing to take on more." He paused. "How about I help out at the commune radio station in the early morning?"

The group leader understood Dabao immediately. Dabao wanted to get up in the morning to learn English when no one was around.

He nodded contently and asked, "Can you get up at 5:30, an hour earlier than others?"

"Yes! I will show up on time every day!" Dabao excitedly answered. To him, it was a piece of cake. It might be extremely difficult for others, as everyone wanted to sleep more during those hard labor days.

Therefore, not to be perceived as a pedant who only knew how to read and apparently admired capitalism, he volunteered to work more during the day and got up an hour earlier than others to read. He did not want to waste his time on entertainment, as learning was his interest. From that day on, Dabao got up in the darkness to go to the commune radio station and set up the devices. Whenever he had extra time, he would practice reading English.

Later, he received praise for his foresight in learning English, but how could he have imagined that English would become a popular tool only a few years later when China reopened its doors to the world in 1977? Like other college students, Dabao learned Russian because China and Russia were comrade countries. He taught himself English out of interest. His father was once fluent in English, and his calligraphy looked like something out of a printed book. Perhaps influenced by his father, Dabao liked literature and foreign languages. He also studied Japanese and later Swedish. Once, he rode an hour to the home of a teacher who taught English on the radio to learn the pronunciation of an English word back when there was no access to the internet or audiotapes.

Dad strived for excellence and concentrated on his research. Having majored in physics in college, he pursued research on low-temperature superconductivity and made great achievements in metal physics. He was interested in various disciplines, including biology, chemistry, material science, medicine, nutrition, the environment, and aviation. He would share new discoveries and inventions in these fields with us over dinner, encouraging my brother and me to become scientists as well. Many of the friends who came to our house were outstanding people in various disciplines, and they often admired Dad's wealth of knowledge, amazed at his interdisciplinary talents. Because of his erudition, he made outstanding achievements in science and technology diplomacy.

Separated from Dad since I was a child, a long separation followed every short meeting. Three times as a child at the age of two, four, and six, I lived with my great-aunt in rural Shijiazhuang because my parents were at cadre schools (countryside labor camps) or under training programs. (When I was eight, Dad left home for a job overseas that would keep him away for six and a half years.) I heard Mom say Dad would come home after sending me away and hold the little clothes I left behind with tears streaming down his face. Men don't easily shed tears, and those days of parting made Dad, a mountain of a man, unable to hold back his tears. In those special and difficult years, there was no other choice but to look forward to a reunion with loved ones.

Occasionally, Dad would bring candy to visit me, which was especially valuable in those days of material scarcity. I remember hiding behind my great-aunt, sizing up this strange father, listening to his gentle words, and wondering if he would take me home this time. After the 1976 Tangshan earthquake, when I was six and my brother nine, our parents sent us to Shijiazhuang again. A few months later, Dad picked up my brother first to go back to Beijing because he was seriously ill.

When I walked them to the end of the village, Dad guiltily told me there were difficulties at home, and he couldn't pick me up this time. He probably said a lot more, but what I remember is he praised me for being strong and obedient. I didn't know what strength was, and it wasn't until after I grew up that I realized my strength came from my parents' encouragement and trust. Just like the song "You Raise Me Up," I am strong when I am on my father's shoulders. He raised me up to more than I could be.

In 1978, Dad went to work in Sweden when I was eight years old, and he could only visit my family once in the next six and half years. At that particular time, Dad had no other choice. But time and space did not separate us, and Dad turned his deep thoughts into individual letters or tapes to each family member every month. His letters were always full of affection.

"Dear daughter, how have you been? You must have grown taller. I miss you so much. I wish I could take you to Zizhuyuan Park for boat rides. Please eat well so you can grow taller and stronger. Please stand tall and keep your back straight. Please help Mom around the house. I believe you are a good girl..."

Dad was very good at telling stories, and the little things became fun when he presented them. The letters he wrote to me were full of interesting facts, which whetted my curiosity and made me fall in love with Sweden.

"Dear daughter, Sweden is a beautiful country with a lot of trees, birds, and fish. During the summer, the days are so long that 8 p.m. is still bright. During the winter, it's the opposite; at 3–4 p.m., it's already dark outside. Snow is as deep as a house. One of my dreams is for you to visit here someday..."

When I was a child, I looked forward to Dad's letters every month, and I was excited to answer them. I told him things that happened to me at home and school. Dad's return letter would praise my improved writing. He would tell me he enjoyed reading my letters, encouraging me to do more exercise and pay attention to my health.

In 2013, thirty-five years later, I finally had the opportunity to visit Sweden for the first time. Dad stayed there from 1978 to 1985, and later on, Mom joined him, working from 1982 to 1985 in this beautiful country I had always dreamed of visiting since I was eight years old. I had planned to bring my parents back to the place where they used to work, but unfortunately, due to illness, they could not make the trip.

I was almost fifteen years old when Dad finally finished his work in Sweden and returned home to us in 1985. Dad always took the time to take us to the parks and talk to us about life. Every time Dad came back from a business trip, he would bring me small gifts—including cute little works of art, books, and toys—and I would cherish them deeply. *The Wonderful*

Adventures of Nils, which my father bought for me, was my favorite book.

In 1987, my parents left for Canada to work. As usual, my brother and I could not follow. Once again, we had a long wait to see each other. At that time, there was no internet, no video, no long phone conversations, only letters to express our longing for each other. Dad's letters were always full of emotion, never preachy, but rather full of genuine encouragement and warmth.

TALENTS AND INFLUENCE

Dad stood tall among his peers in those days, a true giant where most were shorter back then. Standing tall at 1.84 meters (approximately six feet), he earned a spot on the university's varsity basketball team. He proudly represented his school and competed in the prestigious Capital Gymnasium, a renowned sports arena in China. He stressed the importance of physical exercise, practicing shotput with me in middle school and encouraging me to swim, play table tennis, and play badminton. When I was fifteen years old, Dad bought me a pair of roller skates as a gift and practiced with me. In those days, roller skates were a very valuable gift. Nowadays, whenever I rollerblade, fond memories of those beautiful skates and cherished moments with Dad come rushing back.

Dad was a multitalented man, and I loved the crafts he made for me and the little animals he drew. He also wrote beautifully with handsome brush strokes. He had a golden voice, and Mom's enchanting voice was a perfect match. When they got married, they sang "Ao Bao Xiang Hui Love Song" together ("敖包相会"). Hearing them sing it later, I exclaimed that they sounded like our most famous entertainers! Dad taught himself many musical instruments, including piano, violin, erhu, and flute. I often sighed that Dad's intelligence was beyond my reach. His insatiable curiosity and boundless passion for exploring the unknown were truly infectious.

Dad felt guilty for not letting me learn the piano when I was a child because our family was too poor to afford one. Few families could afford it at that time. When my brother was born, my parents had no choice but to sell their beloved violin to buy a crib. Although we didn't have any musical instruments, sounds of singing and reading filled our house. I am grateful for such parents. What more could I ask for?

During my growing-up years, we didn't have much due to money being tight. As time went on and the 1990s brought some improvement, our life remained uncomplicated. Dad taught me a simple life filled with love beats a fancy one without it or with too much distraction. Even now, with plenty of resources in the US, we choose to keep things simple, focusing on relationships over materialism.

From my childhood to adulthood, Dad called me the jewel in the crown and doted on me. On the other hand, I was short-tempered and petulant. Whereas the traditional Chinese father would have berated me, Dad was gentle and always tolerated me, never expressing anger or dissatisfaction with me. Even when I spoke disrespectfully, Dad would not criticize me but forgave me, just as the Bible says, "Do not provoke your children to anger, lest they lose their spirit." When I was bent on making mistakes, Dad would give me space and free will to choose. Well-meaning friends and relatives advised my parents to be tough on my brother and me and not to spoil us so much, but Dad never worried, always saying, "My children are fine and will grow up to be great."

Dad was kind and cheerful and told us stories to inspire us to be excellent and diligent people. I am ashamed to say I did not raise my children in such a wise way. My children can testify to how much I need to learn from Dad.

In previous years, when I struggled with my daughter's adolescent rebellion, Dad listened most patiently to my complaints. Whenever I cried about my child's faults, Dad told me, "She's a good kid. It'll all work out." His tolerance, patience, and faith made me who I became, gave me the courage to grow up, and made me confident and successful. How could I have forgotten all that? He always reminded me, "Love is patient, kind, and gracious." When my daughter didn't go to church, I was so angry and refused to speak to her, yet Dad called her and invited her without accusation, reprimand, or pressure, and just told her, "I miss you, I pray for you, and may God bless you."

When she rejected the invitation, Dad soon invited her back and did not give up. Sometimes, I would get into a heated argument with my child. Afterward, I would regret I had spoken badly and gotten emotional. Dad would comfort me by saying, "How hard it is for you; you are already the best mother in the world."

What heartwarming words! And it made me ashamed! No accusations at all—just praise.

CHAPTER 2

MY MOTHER'S STORY

CHILDHOOD

My mother, Xiaoqin, was born in 1938, the second year after Japan invaded China on a full scale. The Chinese characters mean a little zither, a traditional musical instrument and one of the four arts of ancient Chinese scholars, along with Go (one type of Chinese chess), calligraphy, and painting.

When Xiaoqin was only a couple of months old, her father left home to join the army. His family never heard back from him until four years later, in the unforgiving year of 1942, when he laid down his life as a hero amid the World War II tempest. Even worse, Xiaoqin's mother, his wife, succumbed to poverty and illness shortly after. Left with the cruel weight of loss at the tender age of four, Xiaoqin was thrust into the role of an orphan, struggling in the world of adversity.

"I dreamed about my father so many times. How I wish he could open the door and come home again!" The four-year-old Xiaoqin stared at her grandmother wistfully.

She did not remember seeing her father. She only had some vague memory of her mother.

"Your father was so smart... and very sneaky. He left home without even telling us." Her grandmother sighed.

"Why did he not tell you?" Xiaoqin asked curiously.

"He was the only son in the family. We would not have let him go if we knew," her grandmother answered.

"Your mother did not know either. You were just a baby at that time. How could she let him go?" her grandmother continued.

"Why did he leave us and not come back?" Xiaoqin continued to ask.

"The Japanese killed too many Chinese that year. Your dad heard the news and cried in bed for three days and nights. He was an educated man; young and strong... He sneaked out of the house to join the army that year. He was only seventeen when he left." Her grandmother looked at the sky, trying to hold off her tears.

"We had hoped he would come home after a while. But the news of his death came to us on Lunar New Year's Eve. We were weeping and wailing for the whole day. He was only twenty-one," her grandmother sobbed.

Xiaoqin knew it was time to stop asking questions for the day, even though she enjoyed hearing stories about her parents.

After her mother passed away, she dressed in white for weeks as part of the mourning tradition. A period of mourning can last as long as three years in China. The expectation of people during this time is to be solemn and quiet while they forbid laughter and play. Whenever adults cried and mourned, she had to follow them. Adults told her that her parents' souls were lingering around her while urging her to behave—otherwise, scary ghosts or devils from the underworld might snatch her away.

Fortunately, her grandparents took care of her after her mother died. She followed her grandmother everywhere, helping her feed the chickens, cleaning the yard, and working in the field. Her grandmother mumbled to her again and again about her father. At least she had her grandparents who loved and cared for her. She particularly loved the date tree in the yard, so her grandmother always gave her sweet dates.

She often talked to her grandmother, wishing so deeply her mother was still alive.

"What happened to my mother?" Xiaoqin could not understand how she died so suddenly.

"She was kidnapped by gangsters," her grandmother answered. "They picked on her because there was no man in the house to protect her while your father was fighting the Japanese," her grandmother answered sadly.

"Those bad men wanted money from us. But we did not have any to give. They hit her badly and almost killed her. By the time they brought her back home, she was half dead. No medicine could heal her, and she became bedridden. She died shortly. Poor child..." Her grandmother sighed again. Explaining ransom to a young child was no easy task, yet Xiaoqin seemed to grasp the story. It was scary, but she also felt safe knowing her grandparents were there to protect her.

But good times did not last long.

Years of wars tore the country apart and laid it in rubble as people struggled to live. Not surprisingly, her grandfather fell ill and died in a few years, with her grandmother following not long after. One by one, her loved ones passed away, leaving her to mourn and cry alone.

Since everyone struggled to live during wartime China, Xiaoqin spent her childhood with various families—mostly her aunts and uncles. Her impoverished relatives were just like everyone else, so taking her into their families added burdens. Feeding her whenever food was extremely scarce meant reducing food portions for their own children. Though very young, Xiaoqin understood her position all too well, regarding herself as a burden and an extra. She needed to behave and help out around the house. From a young age, she learned to observe and study others' attitudes and tone of voice, carefully measuring and watching everyone's emotions, language, and gestures to survive. She felt she needed to be good and quiet to please others as she relied on them, believing she was at their mercy. Nonetheless, she was grateful for their kindness in raising her.

At night, she missed her parents and grandparents. It was difficult for her to watch her cousins and friends go to their mothers' beds and cuddle. When other kids called their mom "mama," she followed them by calling their moms "mama," too, which made them laugh at her. She envied those who still had parents around and felt love from them. Even though no one mistreated her or abused her, she wanted a loving family like other children.

Xiaoqin was very ill for one year, and the disease almost killed her. She had fevers on and off for a few months and was too weak to get up from her bed. Some thought she had caught malaria. Since there was no medical care, those who contracted it often died. Adults again told her that her parents were missing her, so they wanted to take her away with them to the underworld. Some lost hope in her. However, miraculously, she found healing after months of struggling. Since she completely recovered without any medicine, the adults were all amazed by it. She survived and learned to be brave and independent. She described herself as a patch of resilient grass that, despite being trampled on, was die-hard.

In 1950, Xiaoqin turned twelve. She received good news in the form of an invitation from one of her aunts—her father's youngest sister. Earlier on, this aunt followed in her brother's footsteps by joining the Chinese guerrillas to fight the Japanese in the 1940s. Along with her husband, she earned awards for their contributions to serving the country after the founding of the New China in 1949, especially during the war of resistance against Japan. They later relocated from the Hebei Province to Beijing to help build the education system in 1950. They gave her the opportunity to continue her education with government subsidies and work at the same time.

Luckily, Xiaoqin's aunt did not forget Xiaoqin. She invited Xiaoqin to Beijing to live with her, an invitation that changed her life forever.

Going to Beijing, a big city, opened her eyes. Everything was new and exciting to her. She found wider roads, cable cars, and tall buildings. The government recognized her father's contribution, so they awarded her a monthly subsidy as an orphan of a martyr who died for the country. The subsidy was meager but just enough to cover her basic living expenses since she was frugal. Also, her aunt was with her, so these changes gave Xiaoqin a sense of security and comfort.

At the same time, she faced new challenges. Previously, she only attended school sporadically because of the wars. Like many orphans, she barely survived and had little opportunity to have any formal education since she lived in a village in the suburbs of Shijiazhuang City. The pain caused by the wars never stymied her enthusiasm for pursuing education. However, she soon found herself in an awkward position as other children had a much better command of academic subjects and general knowledge because they lived in a bigger city and received a better education. They were also more proficient at reading and writing Chinese.

Furthermore, she had a strong accent since she had lived in a small town and couldn't read much initially. Even though she was about to enter middle school, her reading, writing, and math levels were those of an eight-year-old, so she frequently felt embarrassed. In addition, she was not only the shortest but had the weakest physique.

Yet, her determination burned brightly. With no alternatives, she studied day and night to catch up with other children. Like a sponge, she immersed herself in an ocean of books. After one year of hard work, not only did she catch up to her classmates, but she soared past them. On the entrance exam to middle school, her hard work paid off as she attained high scores and received multiple offers from prestigious schools in Beijing.

In high school, she kept up the momentum, performing very well academically. She had two passions, one of which was physics and the other music. The physics teacher praised her highly, telling her: "Physics is a gift of yours. You will have a bright future there. China needs talented people like you in physics. Science and technology will help our country. Go for it!"

After hearing the advice, Xiaoqin's music teacher pleaded with her tearfully to pursue music. "You are so talented at singing. You have a golden voice. It would be a pity if you didn't choose music for your career. I know you love physics, but please consider music…"

The choir Xiaoqin belonged to was the best in the country, receiving an invitation to perform at the radio station in Beijing. Since everyone considered this the highest honor at that time, Xiaoqin had a difficult choice to make.

Ultimately, she chose physics because she enjoyed it whole-heartedly and understood that New China needed to improve in science and technology. Her aunt also encouraged her to pursue physics since it appeared more practical and useful than music.

In 1958, Xiaoqin went to the University of Science and Technology Beijing, formerly known as Beijing Steel and Iron Institute, one of the top universities in China. An outstanding student, she majored in metallurgy physics. In the era of accelerating industrialization and iron and steel production, this university was one of the most sought-after colleges, and only the best students received admission.

ADULTHOOD

In 1958, the first year Xiaoqin attended college, Mao launched a radical campaign to outproduce Great Britain, the mother of the Industrial Revolution, to create a communist utopia. The campaign was known as the "Great Leap Forward" (1958–1962) (Brown 2012). The ambitious goals outlined by the government leaders proved to be far from achievable. To mask the reality of low agricultural output, they would report fabricated records, like inflated harvest yields. As a result, severe food shortages spread throughout the country. While mass starvation largely confined itself to the countryside, urban areas received greatly reduced rations.

At Xiaoqin's college, administrators advised students to return to the dorm to rest right after class was over to reserve energy. The fewer physical activities, the less food one would need. Knowing some students, especially male students, were extremely hungry, Xiaoqin was kind enough to cut down her food purchases so she could save her grain ration tickets and donate them to such students. Being a tiny woman, she knew she had the advantage of not needing too much food, so she was happy to help those in need with her *extra* food ration tickets—even if she experienced hunger as well.

College life was not that easy for Xiaoqin since many students around her were also outstanding and talented. All courses had strict requirements, especially math and physics. Even though the physics department taught math, the curriculum was as rigorous as that of the math department of Beijing University, another top university in China. Xiaoqin put all her energy into her studies and worked even harder than before. Once again, she achieved high scores and became one of the best students year after year.

In 1964, she graduated from college with honors and got assigned to work at a research institute, the same place where Dabao worked as a physics researcher. Coincidentally, it was Dabao who received these new graduates on their first day. As I mentioned in the preceding chapter, it was love at first sight for the young couple when their common interests in physics and music drew them closer together.

In January 1966, Xiaoqin and Dabao got married. That was the first year of the Cultural Revolution, which lasted from 1966–1976. After the Great Leap Forward, political turmoil showed no signs of disappearing, even when the food shortage situation eased. But people were still poor. Xiaoqin and Dabao owned absolutely nothing, not a house, not one piece of furniture because they could not afford any of these. Their only belongings on their wedding day were two small bags—one from each, with clothes, blankets, and books. In addition, Xiaoqin, being the "wealthier" one, had a watch and a violin. The only luxury for celebration was a bag of candies for friends and family on their wedding day. The institute they worked for assigned them a small apartment of about one hundred square feet, not even bigger than half of my current bedroom.

However, Xiaoqin was happy enough. It was her new home, her only home, and above all, her first home. They borrowed a double bed and a desk from the institute.

The bed was a simple wooden structure adorned with a metal frame without a mattress. Even though they bought a new comfortable bed many years later, they still kept the old one at home like a treasure for over fifty-six years.

I used to joke, "Why are you still keeping the old bed, Mom?"

Mom smiled and answered, "It has so many memories. Look, your tooth mark is still on the frame!"

The bed is indeed a treasure. Four generations of us have used it, including my great-aunt, my parents, my brother and me, and my children.

After getting married, they started a simple and happy life together. They dreamed of a better future—raising a couple of kids, supporting Dabao's family, and saving up for furniture, all while singing and enjoying each other's company. To them, this was perfect—a simple life filled with love.

Xiaoqin and Dabao's incomes would have been enough to make them live comfortably without the need to support Dabao's family. But they squeezed every penny so they could save more. Each month, they gave half of their salary to Dabao's mother, grandmother, and younger brother. Toward the end of the month, they could barely save any. Both Dabao and Xiaoqin only had one set of formal clothes for going out to the street for summer and another for winter. It was the same for shoes. The internal layers of Xiaoqin's clothes always had patches, and so did Dabao's because they did not have money for new clothes. Xiaoqin spent a lot of time mending during the evening. In those times, without washing and drying machines, doing laundry meant dedicating a significant portion of the day to wash clothes and wait for them to dry. This laundry day typically fell on Sundays, the only nonworking day. Once, when Dabao's younger brother came to visit, he was surprised by the sight of Xiaoqin's clothes hanging on the line, adorned with so many patches. He exclaimed, "I never knew her clothes had so many patches!" His surprise also hinted at the stark contrast between his relatively less patched clothing and hers. Later on, when life improved in the 1980s, Xiaoqin was able to buy a few more sets of clothes, but she still could not bear to buy new internal layers of clothes for herself.

Xiaoqin and Dabao embraced their patched clothes without care. To them, this simple life woven with love was all they ever wanted.

COURAGE

Another legendary event I heard many times from my parents took place in 1966, namely, the beginning of the unprecedented ten-year Cultural Revolution. Anyone familiar with that history knows how insane and brutal the movement proved toward innocent people. The impact of the Cultural Revolution was devastating, crippling the economy and leaving countless lives shattered. China plunged into a decade of chaos marked by turmoil, bloodshed, hunger, and stagnation. Street violence became common as gangs of students and Red Guards targeted individuals dressed in *bourgeois clothes* while tearing down symbols of *imperialism*. Party officials, teachers, and intellectuals bore the brunt of the upheaval, enduring public humiliation, beatings, and even tragic ends, including murder and suicide, after brutal *struggle sessions*. As Mao ordered security forces not to interfere in the Red Guards' work, blood flowed in Beijing. In August and September 1966 alone, nearly 1,800 people lost their lives in Beijing (Philips 2016).

Xiaoqin's aunt was one of those teachers who were attacked, seized, and tortured by the Red Guards in the school where she worked. They put her in a dungeon, locked and labeled her as an *evil monster*. They allowed no visitors. When Xiaoqin heard about the news, she rushed to the school and requested to visit her aunt.

It was an extremely bold action because she could be persecuted and jailed—a true danger since she was already five months pregnant with her first baby.

When they stopped her at the door of the school, one Red Guard yelled at her and questioned her aggressively. "Who are you? What is your social class?" One's social class was the first topic of interrogation during those times.

Even though Xiaoqin was only five feet tall, she stood straight, looking fearlessly into their eyes, as she answered, "I am the daughter of a hero who died in the war for our country—fighting the Japanese."

Maybe because of her boldness, the Red Guards backed off. Or maybe because her social class belonged to the "Five Red

Categories," which included poor and lower-middle peasants, workers, revolutionary soldiers, revolutionary cadres, and revolutionary martyrs (Yi 2020). They knew from her fierce eyes she was determined to give up her life that day.

They softened their voice. "Who are you visiting? What's the relationship?"

Xiaoqin firmly answered, "I am visiting my aunt. I must visit her now."

They did not further question her and opened the gate for her.

Some of our relatives and friends tried to cut off any relations with people like Xiaoqin's aunt, and even hospitals declined to treat such patients to avoid potential revenge or prosecution, but not Xiaoqin and Dabao. Later, she helped her aunt get medical assistance and cared for her until she fully recovered.

To me, Mom was a heroine for brushing aside her own safety—and no doubt, she was probably the only one who could visit her aunt and appeal for her innocence. But Mom modestly insisted that her advantage boiled down to being the daughter of a hero who died for the country since even gangsters admired heroes.

I asked her many times, "Were you scared when you were stopped by those Red Guards?"

She nodded. "Of course, I was scared inside. I knew it was possible for them to harm me, but I hid my nervousness."

She continued, "I was really concerned since I was pregnant. What if they beat me? But I had no choice. I had no time to think it through and had to prepare for the worst."

"How brave you were, Mom!" I said, feeling so proud of her.

She looked me into my eyes. "It was the right thing to do. My aunt was in danger. How could I not save her?"

She added, "My father was a bold man."

The same bravery ran through her blood.

MOTHERHOOD

One day, as the due date for their first child drew near, Xiaoqin turned to Dabao with a hint of concern in her voice, "I just realized something. We don't have a bed for our baby, and we only have a couple of Yuan left. What should we do?"

Xiaoqin opened the drawer and pulled out an envelope with only a couple of Yuan inside, showing it to him. "Do you think it is possible for us to borrow some money from your mother?"

Dabao shook his head, replying, "No. Mom and Grandmother do not have any extra. They barely make ends meet with the money we give them."

She glanced through her apartment. She did not need to walk to each corner and rummage through the room because the small apartment was only a one hundred square feet studio with one bed, one table, two chairs, and some storage boxes.

Her eyes fixed on her violin and lit up. "How about we sell the violin?"

"No, that's too precious. Besides, it has been yours for many years." Dad shook his head.

"The last time, it was you who played it," Xiaoqin gently reminded him with a smile. It was true that Dabao was a more skilled violinist.

"I was planning to learn and play more, but probably won't have time to. Why let it sit there unused if I don't use it?" Xiaoqin continued.

Together, they decided. The next day, they sold the violin to get twenty Yuan. With that amount, they could buy a small bed for their baby.

Xiaoqin planned to buy it back when she had more money in a couple of years, but she never had enough money. One year after another, her wish faded away.

For the first two years after their first baby was born, Xiaoqin and Dabao were staying at Dabao's mother's home. His mother was taking care of the baby during the day. After work, Xiaoqin returned home to take her baby over so the grandmother could rest. Dabao had to travel to different cities for his projects, so he was too busy to help out at home most of the time.

One day, Xiaoqin came home after work, greeting the grandmother and asking about the baby as usual. Grandmother was a little worried because the baby was fussy for the whole day for some reason. She added that he fell from the bed in the morning. Upon closer observation, Xiaoqin noticed his right arm was bending at an odd angle. When she touched his arm, he immediately withdrew it and cried in pain. She then suspected he had a bone fracture. Carrying him in her arms, she rushed to the hospital. X-ray results validated her suspicion. The baby's wrist was indeed fractured. After treatment, the baby's distress began to subside. By the time they returned home, Xiaoqin was exhausted; without eating, she just wanted to sleep but could not. She had to hold the baby in her arms through the night because he continued to cry from the discomfort of his arm. She could not sleep restfully for many nights.

After a while, Xiaoqin became pregnant again. The pregnancy excited Xiaoqin and Dabao as they were ready to welcome another baby into the family.

It was 1968, the third year after the beginning of the Cultural Revolution. Along with their colleagues, my parents had to attend daily political study and training sessions about Maoism and communism. These sessions were mandatory, and anyone who missed them could face prosecution as a counterrevolutionary criminal.

One morning, Xiaoqin sensed the baby inside of her was less active than before. She wanted to go to the hospital to have her baby checked up by noon but had to focus on the daily political training. As the endless training sessions lasted even longer than usual, she noticed the baby was no longer moving around. After hurrying to the hospital, she received the heart-wrenching news her baby boy had already passed away because the umbilical cord wrapped around his neck. Sorrow filled Xiaoqin, having lost him after seven months of pregnancy.

"How did he look?" Xiaoqin was too upset to look at her baby for long, so she asked Dabao later on.

"Exactly like our oldest son..." Dabao paused and then answered. They grieved for his death for a long time

Mom was super careful when she was pregnant with me. She wanted to make sure nothing would go wrong. Sometimes, she overreacted when she could not sense my movement in her womb. The closer the due date approached, the more anxious Mom became. She rushed to the hospital two days before I was born and had to return home after hearing from the doctor that it was too early. Finally, the day arrived, and I was born without any accidents. My parents were so excited to see me, a healthy girl. The joy I brought to my parents filled the gap in their hearts of losing their second baby. That's another reason they named me *First Ray of the Sunshine*, a symbol of hope, light, and joy.

Mom always put us first and never thought about herself much. She always let me and my brother eat first, leaving the best portion of the meal to us. I remember when I was little, Mom used to prepare scrambled eggs for us every morning: one for my brother and one for me. At that time, however, I never saw her eating any eggs.

Once, I asked her, "Mom, why don't you join us?"

She smiled and admitted, "I want to save them for you. You and your brother are growing fast, so both of you need nutrition. I don't need much."

I continued, "You need it too. You need to grow taller."

Mom laughed, "I won't grow anymore. Why waste food?"

Years later, I realized we used up the limit of our ration card each month, and my brother and I ate Mom's share. That was also when I realized eggs were a luxury.

Mom worked full-time throughout the years. There was a famous quote from Communist Party leader Mao Zedong that "Women hold up half the sky." During the years of the Cultural Revolution—from 1966 to the time of Mao's death in 1976—there seemed to be a sense of freedom and liberation for women (Du 2022). Under that influence, like many women in China, Mom never considered becoming a stay-at-home mom, but in reality, she did most of the housework as the woman of the house. After work, she rushed home to take care of my brother and me.

Because Mom was an outstanding researcher in physics, she did not consider herself a capable mother. She had panic attacks whenever my brother or I got sick. She always believed it was her fault when we were sick.

She told me many times, "My mother left me earlier, so I did not learn how to take good care of you kids. I am sorry..."

She did not know how to sew, knit, or crochet like most of her female friends, nor did she know how to cook like other women or how to decorate and clean the house.

In the mid to late 1980s, our living conditions had improved dramatically. Many families added more variety to the dishes to their tables. Mom envied them and tried to learn from other women. She learned but was still not as proficient. For instance, it took her three hours to make dumplings.

Once, my school organized our fifth-grade classes to rehearse for a performance on stage. Each of the girls would need to wear a red skirt. All my friends had their skirts sewn by their mothers. I knew Mom could not sew a skirt or any clothes for me. I had never seen her do it. She was only able to mend.

Mom offered a solution: "I'll buy you a skirt, just in time for the performance."

In the evening before the performance day, Mom pointed to a bundle of red cloth and elastic bands on the bed, telling me, "I could not find one from shops, so I bought these. I am going to make one for you."

It could be that Mom could not find any red skirts or that she did not have enough money to pay for one.

"Are you sure? I need it tomorrow." I did not understand Mom's concerns at that age. The only thing I cared about was my red skirt.

"Yes, I am a researcher. I promise I will be able to learn and make it for you tonight." Mom lifted up her head, looking at me with a smile.

At the tender age of eleven, I had already surpassed my mother's height. Although she looked so small, I had learned from a young age that my tiny mother had unlimited strength, wisdom, and optimism.

She spent the whole evening drawing on paper, measuring me, and revising her drawing. By 9 p.m., I got tired and went to sleep. Meanwhile, Mom persisted with her task: crafting my red skirt.

The following morning, I arose to a delightful surprise—a beautiful red skirt awaiting me. Mom never shied away from learning new things. Her decision to learn how to sew the red skirt came as a pleasant surprise, though not entirely unexpected, given her intelligence and resourcefulness. Moreover, as years passed, I realized Mom lovingly worked on that skirt, sacrificing her sleep well into the night—a testament to her enduring dedication and love.

RESEARCH

After the Cultural Revolution ended with Mao's death in 1976, China began a period of reform and opening up under Deng Xiaoping, the Chinese paramount leader. The government recognized the importance of scientific and technological development for national progress and initiated an open-door policy to "achieve economic growth through the active introduction of foreign capital and technology while maintaining its commitment to socialism" (Kobayashi, Baobo, and Sano 1999).

Xiaoqin was a high achiever in metallurgy research, especially in the field of duplex steel. Like Dabao, she learned Russian as a second language but not English in college. She had to learn

English in her early forties to read research papers published internationally. That was after the end of the ten-year Cultural Revolution and the beginning of Deng Xiaoping's reform and opening in China. Sweden was among the first countries to sign a bilateral agreement with China on industrial, scientific, and technological cooperation in the 1970s (Fredén 2015).

In 1982, as a distinguished researcher, the KTH Royal Institute of Technology in Sweden selected her to work on a collaborative project. Mom was forty-four years old then. What an honor to be able to work at a world-class institute—a dream of scientific exploration come true! By then, Dabao had already spent four years in Sweden. Xiaoqin missed him dearly throughout this period, and the prospect of going to Sweden also provided a wonderful opportunity for her to reunite with him as he eagerly awaited her arrival.

Nervous and excited, she wondered if she would be able to excel on the new project since she had never traveled to a foreign country or learned English formally. She was also worried about my brother and me. Because the country was still relatively poor in the early 1980s, children could not accompany their parents to foreign countries. I was twelve, and my brother was fifteen, so we still needed our parents' guidance and companionship. She hesitated. Would she give up this opportunity for her children? It was her aunt who stood up to support her, fortunately, as she encouraged Mom to seize the opportunity. She decided to move to our apartment to take care of us during Mom's absence.

On the day before Mom's departure for Sweden, Mom and I walked back home after our shopping. The summer sun blazed in the sky, and the air was heavy with the persistent hum of cicadas, making even breathing a challenge.

"Will you eat well and sleep well when I am gone?" she asked me.

We don't say *love* in Chinese culture. When people remind you to eat, it's a way of expressing care and affection.

"I will. Don't worry about me. I am a big girl now," I replied, pretending I did not care about her impending departure.

"And when will you return?" I asked, though I understood she might not know the answer.

"Maybe in one year or two," she replied, searching for the right words.

"Fine, two years it is. Keep this with you so you will remember it." I plucked one dog's tail grass by the road and handed it to her.

Mom nodded. "Yes, I promise. And you promise to write me letters… You take good care of yourself. Help your great-aunt around the house. Okay?"

In August 1982, tears welled up in Mom's eyes as she bid us farewell. She had a greater mountain to climb ahead of her.

The trip to Sweden took her an entire week by train. Taking an airplane was too costly, so all the scholars from her working institute traveled by train. To save money on buying food, Mom packed dry food for the seven-day journey.

The research in Sweden was hard for her, especially with language and culture barriers. But she never gave up. She spent day and night reading research papers, experimenting with new tools, and building math models.

"It was very difficult for the first three months. I could not even understand what the scope of the project was," Mom told me many years later.

"My English was not good enough to engage in discussions with my professor, even though he was very kind and patient. I felt embarrassed for asking so many questions, especially my broken English," she continued with a wry smile.

"What did you do to get used to it then?" I asked her.

"I had to become bold. I had to ask him without being too shy. After a while, I was able to discuss more freely with my professor. One day, he was surprised I could even contribute new ideas to the project." Mom relaxed a little bit.

"Did he think you were not a good researcher?" I was interested in knowing it.

"He might be disappointed at the beginning. The important thing was I had confidence in myself," she continued.

"As long as I put in more hours, I believe I can always improve and adapt. Actually, I put extra hours into my project. When everyone went home around 5 p.m., I stayed in the lab to work at least another two hours, plus weekends." She was obviously proud of her hard work.

During the winter, she went to work before dawn and watched the moon rise when she came home. From her new residence to the research institute, the commute took an hour by train. She usually read papers and took notes on the ride. At the same time, she had to watch the station. The signs and announcements were only in Swedish, so there were several times when she missed her station and had to take another train to return. She had to figure out how to count the number of stations to accurately locate herself.

In her letter, she told me she befriended a woman who was studying under the same professor.

"Her name is Margaret. She was young, tall, and beautiful. She used to play volleyball for the Sweden National Team. She started studying under our professor after her retirement from the volleyball team." She wrote.

In the next letter, Mom told me more about her new friend. "She had one small girl, a two-year-old. She is pregnant and about to have her second baby... I helped her a lot with her research paper. She also helped me tremendously with my project. We always need our friends no matter what."

Mom and Margaret collaborated on a project, and their efforts made the project successful. Margaret helped Mom with the equipment and tools she never got to use in China, while Mom helped her with mathematic models. Mom's solid knowledge of physics and math helped her to push the project forward.

I did not understand all the terminology in the metallurgy areas that Mom talked about, such as fracture mechanics and duplex steel, but only remembered she had to perform lots of tests, adjustments, and measurements again and again.

"For example, to test the properties of the copper alloy under different conditions, I needed to design the test, including temperature, pressure, etc., predict its reaction, and measure its characteristics." She shared it with me once.

"I had to sand the alloy very thin and very evenly. Making it very thin took hours. Sometimes, it was too thin and broke. I had to start it over again," she explained to me.

"Was there a machine that could help you?" I asked.

"Not really. In the future, might be... I had to be very careful sanding it. The closer to the end, the harder... The alloy was so thin that it could be almost transparent, and light could go through..." Mom answered and shared with enthusiasm even years later.

Her passion for metals and research was undeniable, evident in the roughened skin of her hands from countless hours spent in the lab. She joked that her fingers were short and sturdy, and they were obviously *working people's hands*—a term perceived as a virtue in China. To convert *pampered scholars* into working people, they sent intellectuals to the cadre school and remote harsh farmland for reeducation during the Cultural Revolution.

Another challenging aspect of her time in Sweden was adjusting to the local food options. Since vegetables were very expensive, she had to carefully plan her purchases around available sales. Mom was lactose intolerant, but a lot of meals had dairy ingredients, which caused her stomach to ache all the time. She had to be careful in selecting and consuming food.

With her hard work, she earned many awards and recognition. Among her notable achievements was the simplification of an empirical equation, a complex formula originally developed by her professor years ago. Back then, computers and calculators didn't exist, so Mom dedicated countless days to manual calculations based on her research and experiments. She'd chuckle as she recalled the mountains of paper she'd used, stacks that could easily fill several towering boxes up to the ceiling. Her professor could not believe her equation was correct at the beginning. Mom proved it to him with test data and calculation processes. Ultimately, her professor's endorsement came in a celebratory declaration before the entire department, praising Mom as a brilliant, industrious, and resilient researcher.

Her professor invited her to stay and extend her research for an additional year. She could have earned her PhD if she continued working there for another year. She had already passed the two-year mark she promised me. In 1985, she returned home after having dedicated nearly three years to her academic pursuit. All these achievements were nothing compared to the feeling of missing her children. She wrote many letters to us, full of love and care. In her heart, the pursuit of a PhD faded to insignificance in comparison to the cherished moments she wished she could share with us.

Her example resonates deeply within me, teaching the boundless capacity of a mother's love. As she once shared with me, "A mother's devotion knows no bounds."

FAMILY REUNION

Our family finally reunited in 1985 after a lengthy seven-year separation. Time had etched its marks upon Mom—gray strands wove into her hair, and she had shrunk too. She used to hide these hairs before the trip to Sweden, but now she did not care much. What truly mattered was she had her family back together again, which brought her indescribable joy.

With our reunion, we moved to a more spacious three-bedroom apartment. The additional space brought a busier routine for Mom, yet her contentment radiated through her bustling activity. Once more, the familiar hum of her favorite songs reverberated throughout our home, reminiscent of happier days. Meanwhile, I advanced to a new high school, and my brother ventured into college life. Mom and Dad resumed their former roles but embarked on fresh projects, further dedicating themselves to their beloved careers in science. After enduring years of separation and upheaval, a sense of tranquility enveloped us, and the air was filled with the sweet symphony of togetherness.

However, as is often the case in reality, our season of happiness proved short-lived. How I wished our life had a fairytale-like ending with the declaration of *happily ever after*.

One day, I inadvertently overheard a serious conversation between Mom and Dad.

"I need to have surgery soon. It is to remove *everything*—hysterectomy surgery." Mom's voice carried the weight of concern.

Dad's tone softened, "What do you mean by everything?"

"Uterus and ovaries—everything, because of my uterine fibroids." Mom's words came out in a hushed whisper. "The doctor suspects it might be a malignant tumor."

A brief silence hung in the air.

"How soon?" Dad inquired.

"Next week. You should still go on your trip. I will be fine," Mom reassured Dad, her voice gentle.

Another moment of quiet followed.

Fortunately, Mom's surgery was successful, and her tumor turned out to be benign.

Dad departed for his trip the day after Mom returned home from the hospital. His restless nights were evident, but as morning broke, Mom's smile conveyed her assurance of a swift recovery.

However, the road to recovery stretched out, and the process was agonizing.

For some reason, the doctor did not prescribe her strong painkillers, leaving her to grapple with extreme pain in bed. Her surgery forced her body to enter into menopause abruptly. The magnitude of the change caught her off guard. Later on, she learned she developed arrhythmia and heart palpitations. The doctor was not sure about the cause of her heart problems. Mom remained convinced the surgery ignited her heart issues.

Most days, Mom lay on her bed quietly staring at the sunshine streaming through the window during the day while I attended school. I'd assist her in changing clothes and sheets when her sweating became too much. Daily, I would prepare her breakfast and dinner. I centered my teenage focus on homework, friends, and molding my self-image—the quintessential self-absorbed teenager. Regrettably, my attentiveness toward Mom was minimal, and our interactions were scarce. Through it all, Mom never uttered a complaint or criticized me. On the contrary, she consistently expressed her gratitude for my care, acknowledging her days would have been far more arduous and painful without it.

One day, Mom looked better, lying on her bed. The setting sun shone on the wall next to her bed, making her look extraordinarily fragile and petite.

"Are you still in pain?" I asked gently, noticing the sweat on her forehead.

"Nothing major. You get busy with your own work... when will your dad come home?" Mom inquired.

"He'll return in another week," I replied, aware of his three-week trip.

Her question revealed her yearning for Dad's presence. After all the years of self-sufficiency, this was the only time she allowed herself to appear vulnerable in front of me.

Mom's eyes shimmered with emotion when Dad finally returned the next week, and tears welled up in her eyes.

Observing her fragile form on the bed, her pale face, and her tears, Dad regretted he did not stay with Mom to take care of her when she needed him the most.

Dad confided in Mom, "It hurt me to the core." The two Chinese characters Dad used, "Xin Teng," 心疼, are a unique combination that holds a profound meaning. *Xin* means heart, while *Teng* means pain. So, literally, it is "I very much heartache you," meaning, "You make my heart ache so much." My family commonly uses these two characters. It expresses deep love, even though we never said "love" to each other. When witnessing our loved ones in distress, we convey our feelings by saying, "I heart ache you." Countless times, Mom and Dad have shared this sentiment with me throughout my life.

Dad openly admitted that embarking on his trip during such a critical period was one of his most regrettable decisions.

Three years after Mom's hysterectomy surgery, in 1988, Mom battled serious shingles and once again displayed remarkable resilience, a trait that defined her. When Dad faced wrongful accusations and betrayal at work in 1991, she stood beside him, offering steadfast emotional support until ultimately vindicating his innocence a year later. These anecdotes are just a glimpse into the countless challenges Mom faced. Throughout, she always kept her spirit elevated, overcoming every difficulty with her noteworthy resilience.

Mom has been my role model, and she is always my inspiration. Her resilience, optimism, and independence have left an indelible mark on me. Her mantra, "Nothing can beat me down," echoes resolutely in my heart. Amid her own trials, she instilled in me a sense of compassion for the vulnerable and downtrodden. Her life, marked by hardships, has only fueled her desire to extend a helping hand to those in need.

FAREWELL TO DAD

I was holding Mom's hand on the day, standing in front of the burial site of my father in Jan 2022. Mom was already an old woman of eighty-three years old. Her hunched back and scoliosis made her look shorter than before. The cold winter wind blew up her gray hair. I watched her wiping off tears from her face. Her hand was shaking.

From years of pressing and handling machine tools and metals, her fingers had become rough—her fingerprints became unrecognizable by the fingerprints machine. Those were the hands that sewed me the red skirt. Those were the hands that made dumplings for three hours. Those were the hands that touched my forehead hundreds of times. She is one of the most resilient and optimistic people I have ever known. "There's always hope." That's what I hear from her all the time.

CHAPTER 3

MY CHILDHOOD AND IMMIGRATION STORIES

———

TANGSHAN EARTHQUAKE

It was July 28, 1976. Beijing, China. "Get up! Run!" Mom's yelling woke me up suddenly. Bang! Loud noises mixed with the sounds of babies crying filled the hallway outside of our apartment. I was shocked and froze there. My nine-year-old brother rolled out of our bunkbed immediately, and the bed continued to shake. He tumbled, got up, and rushed to the door.

Overwhelmed by fear, I burst into tears. At that moment, Dad reached out to lift me up and quickly carried me outside. In front of us, the crowded pitch-dark stairway was already crowded. Within seconds, we stumbled to the first floor and then outside. Mom's panicking eyes searched for my brother and finally relaxed after seeing him. She took me into her warm arms and sighed, "We just escaped the earthquake. We are lucky." I didn't think I was lucky because I did not even have my shoes on. The fortunate one was my brother.

He was the first one to run out of the building and gather with his friends.

I did not realize until later that I had just experienced the Tangshan earthquake, one of the deadliest earthquakes of the twentieth century, which killed over half a million people in China and shook the country that had already suffered deeply from the political turmoil (Rafferty 2023).

The earthquake mildly damaged our apartment building in Beijing, making cracks in the wall, but no one dared to stay inside afterward. Many set up large tents with plastic tarps as temporary shelters, and we all moved in. Everything seemed gloomy, and people were depressed. Mom comforted us, saying we were lucky because we had a place to stay, and life would be better tomorrow. Her optimism encouraged all of us. But to me, my brother was even luckier. He was strong and tall enough to carry the water bucket used to receive rainwater from the leaky roof. He also volunteered to run back to our home to pick up some clothes, regardless of the possibility of life-threatening aftershocks. After all, he was three years older than I was. He was fearless, and I admired him.

Luckily, the tragedy happened during the summer; otherwise, it would have been worse in the winter with the wind and snow.

I trusted Mom, and life was indeed wonderful. I not only had a chance to play with my friends during the day but also ate and slept with them at night. Living in the shelter was like camping every day. The most enjoyable activity was listening to the scary ghost stories in the dark while shaking and screaming together with other kids underneath blankets. I think those stories first sparked my storytelling ability.

After living on the street for a couple of weeks, my parents decided it would be better for my brother and me to live with LaoLao, my great-aunt. LaoLao means grandma in Chinese. She was my mother's aunt who lived in a remote village in Hebei Province. When Mom lost her parents and grandparents, for a period of time, she lived with LaoLao, one of the few closest relatives.

We took a four-hour train ride from Beijing to LaoLao's place. Mom took my brother and me to my great-aunt and introduced us to all the relatives in the room there. I held Mom's hand tight, hoping she would take me home with her. I knew she had made up her mind, but what if she changed her mind? I tried my best to behave and be an obedient girl that day. Perhaps she would take pity on me and bring me home.

Saying goodbye to her was one of my hardest moments. I knew she would return home and leave me there, so I refused to close my eyes during the night. Again and again, Mom urged me to go to sleep.

I told her, "No. I know you will leave me when I close my eyes." Based on my previous experiences, she left me while I was asleep each time she sent me to Shijiazhuang.

She smiled and comforted me by saying, "I promise. I won't leave you."

She would repeat it multiple times until I felt exhausted and fell asleep. In the morning, I got up and realized she was gone.

Upset and quiet, I sighed, knowing she lied to me again. I was angry at myself for having fallen asleep last night. LaoLao called all her four grandchildren over to play with my brother and me. I was happy they were all girls around my age.

In that rural landscape, life was spartan. Only limited amounts of medicine and food were available. Rice and steamed buns were a rarity, while meat or eggs tasted like a luxurious indulgence. Of course, there was no TV, movies, or books. Our toys were only rocks, dirt, and twigs. Winter always left my hands chapped, but the contentment of slumbering on the fire bed, known as the Kang—a wide bed built from mud and brick with a stove beneath to keep us warm, was enough to melt away any discomfort. I was able to adapt to my new life quickly.

I envied and admired my brother for being taller, stronger, and smarter. He could read and write and knew many more ghost stories than I did. I, on the other hand, seemed to be a perpetual sufferer of sickness while my brother remained healthy and vibrant. What's more, he could carry me on his back all the way from the bus station to our home in Beijing when Mom was too weary to bear my weight. Even though he called me "spoiled," he still carried me on his back whenever I begged him.

However, luck wasn't on his side this time. A change in living conditions rendered him persistently unwell. There were no medical facilities in the village. Finally, my brother fell too ill to get up, so he spent the whole day in bed. Boys his age should be full of energy, jumping and playing. Concerned about his well-being, LaoLao wrote a letter to my parents to urge them to take him to Beijing for diagnosis and treatment. Dad finally arrived after a few days. I was excited, hoping he would take both of us back. The next day, we walked to the bus stop at the end of the village.

After expressing gratitude to LaoLao, Dad turned his attention to me and said gently, "You need to go back with LaoLao. I will take your brother home."

"I want to go with you. I want to take the bus home too." I stepped up closer to him.

Dad bent over to speak to me with a soft voice. "There are difficulties at home. You will stay here. You are a good girl."

I did not understand what *difficulties* meant. I was thinking how lucky my brother was! I was jealous of him. I wished I was that sick so Dad could take me with him.

Observing my skinny body and runny nose due to an infection, Dad was reluctant to leave me there. I imagine he must have been sad as he tried to comfort me. I remember he said, "You are a tough and brave girl." That suddenly lifted my spirits.

My brother outshone me in every aspect, at least in my young eyes. However, this time, I beat him. I was no longer jealous of him because I was the tough and brave one. While the separation from Mom and Dad tugged at my emotions, tears did not flow, for I had evolved into the resilient one. With Mom and Dad's trust and praises encouraging me, I found solace, and amid the trials, I stood steadfast, unburdening them with the weight of worry.

Furthermore, the candies my dad brought me from Beijing provided comfort to me. They became an instant sensation, captivating all the kids in the neighborhood. For many, it was the first time they had tasted candy, and the simple flavor brought a sensation etched into their memories for a lifetime. "Do you want some candy?" Whenever I opened my dirty palm with candies, their eyes opened wide, sparkling with awe. I could immediately feel the envy and respect from the kids around me. Oh, how lucky I was! That winter was super long and cold. I endured the hardships of rural life and also won many friends with these sweet treats. As I reflect on those times, with the unwavering love from my parents and the care of LaoLao, along with the loyal friendships, can I not consider myself fortunate?

CHILDHOOD ACTIVITIES

Mom often reflected on how challenging it was to raise me due to my frequent illnesses. Allergies to various foods led to digestion issues and persistent stomach aches. I also had occasional low blood sugar problems that caused me to faint. Eventually, Mom found out I had been placed on the blacklist of the childcare centers in the neighborhood—my fainting startled the staff. This became another factor in my parents' decision to send me to my great-aunt's home in Shijiazhuang, not once, but three times before I reached the age of seven.

I was prone to passing out and hitting my head on the ground, which terrified people around me. Therefore, Mom taught me to squat or sit down whenever I felt dizzy. I learned that lowering my body would redirect the blood flow to my head, preventing me from passing out. Along with this coping mechanism, she would pack me one candy in my pocket as a snack. However, my elementary school prohibited bringing any food to school, so I had to hide my candies. Therefore, I discovered that sitting down was the most effective way to combat my dizziness.

During the time living with my great-aunt, the most embarrassing thing was not my health but rather my lack of familiarity with farm-related tasks. Growing up away from farmland, I wasn't as adept at these chores as my neighborhood companions.

One daily school task was to scoop up the grains after the adults collected the wheat from the field. At the end of the day, we submitted the grains to the school, and the teacher would mark the weight of the grains collected. I vividly recall I collected the smallest amount among all the children. In the evening, one relative asked me how much I collected for the day. With a heavy heart, I tearfully replied, "Only two Liang" (about 3.5 ounces). He patted me on the back, trying to comfort me, though my tears continued to flow. Then, one of my beloved cousins rushed over, clasping my hand. She whispered that she would share some of her harvests the following day so I wouldn't be last. The next day, she offered me two Liang of her collection, making my share not as meager as the previous day. It was a much brighter day for me, and I deeply felt grateful for her help.

Another challenging task was to collect manure, which often resembled soil, especially when it was dry and flattened on the dirt road. Even though I was six, I could not even compete with four-year-olds who grew up in the countryside. They had seen manure almost daily from birth, so they were familiar with it. As a result, any manure I spotted was swiftly claimed by others who had a quicker eye and faster legs. I sighed. I came back to school empty-handed, feeling discouraged.

One neighborhood girl shared a trick with me, "You've got to go to the gate of the stable." She showed me I could find more manure there. All horses, mules, and donkeys returned to the same place at the end of the day. She and I waited till they showed up by the evening. They always left dung on the ground by the gate. Just before the adults began cleaning up after the animals, we quickly gathered all the manure. Success finally came our way! I was truly grateful for my friend's guidance, which made all the difference.

Food was scarce in rural areas, leaving everyone equally hungry. I developed a fondness for the fresh vegetables found in the fields—cucumbers, tomatoes, and eggplants—which tasted surprisingly delightful when eaten raw. Nowadays, people stress the importance of eating multigrain bread, yet during that time, our diets were mainly composed of coarse grains. Corn flour, with its substantial grains, stood out as the prevalent coarse grain; on the other hand, rice and flour were rare commodities, appearing on our table only during festive occasions. Regrettably, a recurring issue was that these sustenance options merely provided temporary satisfaction before my stomach growled again.

My great-aunt made the most delicious steamed buns out of corn grains. The best meal was sizzling steamed buns with pork oil, along with green onions and wood ears collected from logs in the nearby woods. Upon my return to Beijing,

I was pleasantly surprised to discover every meal featured either rice or steamed flour buns. Such a treat felt like a feast to me—a true indulgence!

I did not like winter because I had to bundle up with layers of thick pants while my nose was still congested. But the worst thing was the cold, which dried and roughened the skin on the back of my hands such that they would bleed painfully. All the children around me also had cracked hands. My great-aunt, resourceful as ever, knew how to heal wounds using magic powder derived from a wooden door bolt. Yet, this powder's enchantment lay solely in treating injuries, not parched skin. Instead, she advised me to wash my hands and apply a coat of cooking oil to the skin. But I felt too cold and refused to wash my hands. I only washed my hands before meals.

Our water source was a well, its contents hoisted using a bucket. The water, stored in a cylindrical ceramic tank within our house, served all our needs—for drinking, cooking, and washing. Since the house was freezing cold, so was the water. This only deepened my aversion to handwashing. Luckily, my great-aunt possessed a copper water basin for handwashing, designed in the shape of a cowboy hat. I had a fondness for it, likely because she did too.

The village children and I were adept at finding amusement in the simplest things. We engaged in ice skating using regular shoes, as the notion of ice skates eluded us entirely. Snow became our playground, and one of my cherished pastimes involved crafting a shaker. This creative endeavor started with putting one or two small stones inside a snowball before using mud to wrap around the snowball to make it sturdy. After drying the mud ball in the sun for a couple of days, the snow would melt away, leaving only the dirt-clad ball with the stones inside. While my attempts usually ended in cracked dirt balls, the process was brimming with enjoyment and hope, fueled by the aspiration of crafting the finest shaker in the village.

To my young eyes, my great-aunt was the most brilliant person in the world. She skillfully managed every aspect of our household and yard—cooking, gardening, poultry rearing, and more. Her talents extended not only to nursing me back to health but also to tending to the well-being of our chickens. At one time, one of the hens wobbled in the yard like a drunken person. My great-aunt told me chemical fertilizers or pesticides must have poisoned her.

She observed the hen for a few minutes and told me it would die without treatment. The hen was one of my favorites, which always produced eggs. It would have been a pity to watch her die. My great-aunt decided to perform surgery; she put the hen on her lap and then used a pair of scissors to cut open the hen's neck and take out all the food inside. Afterward, she quickly and skillfully sewed up her neck and stomach within a minute or so. The hen's blood streamed down, and it looked dead. My great-aunt then fed the hen some water and let it lay there for a while. After a couple of hours, the hen slowly got up and looked and moved around before returning to her normal self, walking around, cooing, and searching for food in the yard along with other chickens. It lived for another year. When I grew older, I thought about the surgery. I wondered if it was the proper method of treating a poisoned chicken. I could not find the right answer, even after searching the internet. Nonetheless, since I had actually witnessed the surgery, I couldn't help but trust my great-aunt performed the surgery successfully. My admiration for her deepened as I marveled at her resourcefulness and courage.

My great-uncle was my maternal grandmother's brother. My great-aunt married him, so my great-aunt had no blood relationship with my mom, which, by extension, meant she and I had no blood connection either. Yet, this fact did not impact her boundless affection for me. Despite her limited formal education, she possessed a wealth of wisdom and shared captivating folklore with me in the softest voice. When I was just a child, she patiently taught me how to count numbers, marveling at how quickly I grasped the pattern of counting by tens. She had bound feet, an image often seen in documentary films. I saw her wrapping and unwrapping her feet each day since I slept with her on the same Kang (i.e., a large, heated bed made of bricks). From the early twentieth century up to the 1940s, foot binding was a part of Chinese culture. Imagine how hard it was for women who toiled in the fields and at home. She planted two pear trees in the yard. During the harvest season, she would always give me more pears. Even in the midst of the challenge of dividing the fruit among her four grandchildren, she made sure I had an additional piece. Sometimes, she hid it from the other children and gave it to me when they left.

Numerous trials marked my great-aunt's life, each hardship more challenging than the last. She bore the heart-wrenching pain of losing six of her ten children at young ages due to poverty, illnesses, and wars. The early 1970s brought yet another blow with the passing of her husband. Despite this cascade of tragedies, she never surrendered to bitterness or despair. Instead, she became an unyielding pillar of strength for her family.

Though not exceeding two years in total, my time spent in Shijiazhuang remains one of the most cherished periods of my childhood. The constant battles with illness taught me the importance of nurturing my own well-being. I also learned to be optimistic every day, hoping to reunite with my parents. Fortunately, throughout the whole time, I could lean on my great-aunt, who was one of the kindest souls I'd ever known.

The last time I saw her was during my visit to the village in the summer after I graduated from high school. Everything changed so much, and I could not remember anything from my childhood days. The only thing that remained was the radiant smile of my great-aunt. She was excited to see me after thirteen years and prepared a special lunch for us on that hot and humid day. Regrettably, I forgot to bring a camera with me, so I could not take a picture with her. How I wish I had captured that moment, frozen in time with her beside me. It was a day etched into my memory as our final encounter. The course of life would lead me to speak to her only once more, a year preceding her death.

As I look back, the influence of my remarkable great-aunt continues to guide my journey, reminding me of the power of optimism, resilience, and unwavering kindness.

GLORIOUS FOOD

I heard the song "Food, Glorious Food" from my daughter, who was a choir member in her school. The song depicts a scene where half-starved orphan boys in nineteenth-century London are dreaming and fantasizing about food. For me, however, the song would invoke scenes of Three Years of

Great Chinese Famine or Three Years of Natural Disasters from 1958 to 1961.

I was always curious about how Dad donated his food rationing coupons to a sick friend because many times I heard him saying that the rice coupons were so precious and never seemed enough. He answered me with a smile, "Skip meals, no other tricks." He continued, "I was able to save several kilograms for that student at the end of the month, every month."

Ten years later, I was fortunate enough to be born after the country recovered from the Three-Year Disaster. However, the nightmare of starvation still haunted those who had survived since food shortage was still a primary concern. One of my friends, a few years older than me, once confided that he still refuses to eat sweet potatoes despite their rich fiber and vitamins, all because of the memories from his childhood. Sweet potato soup, boiled sweet potatoes, sweet potato porridge, and sweet potato leaves were the staples imprinted in his recollections.

My family was in a relatively better situation, but memories of running out of money from time to time remain vivid. I can still recall those moments when Mom anxiously awaited her monthly salary. There were instances when she had to ask me to collect and recycle soy sauce bottles to scrape together five or ten cents to buy food by the end of the month. Both my brother and I took turns waiting in the lengthy queue at the grocery shop to buy meat. Those buying under half a Yuan of pork required no rationing card. My brother bought a mere half Yuan worth, around a small stripe of less than half a pound. Then, I made the same purchase, followed by my brother repeating the process. This cycle continued, allowing us to accumulate more meat over several rounds.

Eggs served as our primary source of nutrition, and yet Mom refrained from eating them, keen on saving them for us. One day, I mentioned to a Chinese friend that during my childhood, I used to consume one egg per day. His response caught me by surprise: "Wow. That was luxury! Back then, I only had a chance to eat eggs during Chinese New Year, birthdays, or other special occasions. You folks were so fortunate!" His words left me utterly speechless.

MY IMMIGRATION STORIES

"You don't want to move to that ghost room. Feng Shui there is not good. Two people who lived there died tragically." My UCLA friend who also came from China, warned me. "The first person took her own life. The second person died in a car accident last year. Both were Chinese girls. The room seems cursed."

I responded with conviction, "I am not superstitious. I simply want to switch to another dorm room—a double unit, to be able to focus on my studies."

It was September 1995, one week before the beginning of the first semester at UCLA. I was sharing a room with two other women in the co-op apartment. With the goal of completing the graduate program within a year, I needed an environment where I could concentrate solely on my studies. So, I applied to switch to a double unit. As a new student, I was at the bottom of the waiting list for housing assignments. Despite the pessimism of those around me, I decided to apply anyway, holding onto the hope of a miracle. God answered my prayers when, just two days later, I received notification no one else wanted that *ghost unit*. I seized the opportunity and moved in, now sharing the unit with a Vietnamese woman who hadn't heard the unsettling story of the "ghost unit."

Before attending UCLA, I needed to ensure I had enough funds to cover my living expenses. Fortunately, I received a scholarship that would cover my tuition. Thus, I worked at a Chinese restaurant over the summer. After this, I managed to save around $1,000, a sum I found quite satisfactory. With an additional $1,000 contributed by my parents and $1,000 earned from my job in China, I had a total of $3,000 in my account, which I budgeted for my graduate program. This budget translated to an average monthly expenditure of $300, including rent, food, and all other expenses, assuming I could finish my graduate program within one year. I had the determination to be extremely thrifty.

The desire to complete my graduate degree within a single year and thus economize fueled my dedication to my studies. As the 1996 school year concluded, I realized my dreams had come to fruition, all while following my $3,000 budget. I was fortunate to have received considerable assistance from my professors and friends along the way.

CULTURE AND LANGUAGE BARRIER
By nature, I'm a talkative person and a storyteller who enjoys sharing her thoughts on a daily basis. However, coming to America paused my desire to tell stories because of the

language barrier. Expressing my feelings and describing facts accurately required a conscious effort to search for the right words, which often left me feeling drained. At times, I refrained from speaking simply due to the uncertainty within me.

While I could hold conversations, they fell short of the level I aspired to. I wanted to talk about sports, culture, arts, politics, movies, books, and food. I was also aware that my knowledge of America and the Western world was so limited. Who would want to chat with me if work and basic greetings were my limited topics? For example, one colleague mentioned his favorite band was the Grateful Dead. I had no idea what that meant. I was an avid soccer fan and wished to discuss the legendary Argentine soccer star Maradona, but no Americans around me recognized his name. The impeachment of President Clinton baffled me, but my hesitation held me back from asking questions. I couldn't comprehend how he was still a president after his impeachment, resulting in an affair with Monica Lewinsky that became public.

Despite having studied English from middle school through college, I felt quite inadequate when I first arrived in this country. Certain words always seemed to blend together for me, such as *desert* and *dessert, soup* and *soap, monk* and *monkey, kitchen* and *chicken*. Imagine the embarrassment I encountered through the years.

For instance, when I enrolled as a graduate student at UCLA, I called the dormitory to ask about the availability of the room and rental price. Being curious about the layout of the dorm, I asked him, "Is there a *chicken* in the room?" There was a moment of silence on the other side of the phone line, and then he answered: "Sorry, I don't understand your question." Suddenly, I realized my mistake. "Oh, so sorry, I meant to ask you if there is a *kitchen* in the room." I heard him quietly answer, "No, ma'am. No kitchen or chicken either." That was so embarrassing!

Even more embarrassing was how I always confused *she* and *he*. That's because, in spoken Chinese, there's no distinction between genders. Sometimes, I referred to a boy as *she*, a girl as *he*, or the husband of a couple as *her, she,* or *his husband*. Invariably, perplexed stares met those moments.

I felt nervous when ordering food at restaurants. Once, perusing the menu, I came across an item labeled *fish fingers*. Being curious and brave, I asked the waiter about the type of fish. The waiter answered me quickly, but I could not relate it to a Chinese term. I decided to order it to see what kind of fish has fingers. How disappointed I was to find no fingers at all! They were just nuggets for us to eat with our fingers. Feeling so cheated, I used my fork to eat the fish fingers. Mm, fish fingers tasted better than the fish itself. From that day on, I learned I could no longer trust the name.

Then there was the time when I was traveling in Louisiana and went to a nice restaurant. When I saw *alligator burger* on the menu, I thought, "Don't trick me this time. They must have shaped the burger like an alligator." So, I ordered it, and it did not look like an alligator at all but tasted good. It was only later I discovered I had enjoyed alligator meat. Imagine that! In my wildest dreams, I'd never have thought of devouring the fearsome creature. I always assumed it would be the other way around. I was immensely proud of myself afterward. From that day on, I took every opportunity to boast in front of my Chinese friends, "Guess what? I ate an alligator in America!"

Also, I felt frustrated with the American accent and talking speed. Having learned British English back in China, American English felt like an entirely different language. For example, people pronounce *garage*, *tomato*, and *kilometer* differently, and that confused me a lot. I did not (and still don't) understand why the US adhered to the old English measuring system when nearly the whole world has adopted the metric system. With the US using miles instead of kilometers, Fahrenheit instead of Celsius, feet instead of meters, and gallons instead of liters, I often felt lost. On one occasion, when someone asked about my height, I responded, "I'm 1.64 meters," this caused confusion, leading her to request a conversion into feet and inches. Caught off guard, I paused and eventually said, "I'm five feet ten inches." That obviously surprised her, so she sized me up and down. Later on, I realized 1.64 meters is equivalent to 5'5". Such moments were a reminder of the challenges of navigating measurement differences across cultures.

MY FIRST AMERICAN FRIEND
Beth held the distinction of being my very first American friend when I arrived in the US back in 1994. I landed an internship position at a nonprofit organization where she was the office manager. In those early days, my spoken English was quite rudimentary, and my shyness was evident. However, Beth's warm welcome and assistance played a significant role in helping me find my footing within the office. She patiently

explained to me the organization's mission, in which we offer information about different cancer treatment methods to its members. My specific role involved creating and managing a database for the members while also generating reports tailored to their requirements. This role essentially combined elements of a database administrator, a data analyst, and a tech support specialist. As the days progressed, I began to master the responsibilities of the role, thanks in no small part to Beth's guidance and support.

She is one of the nicest and most gracious people I have ever met. Since she was around the same age as my parents, I always felt she was like a second mother to me. She always asked me whether she could help me with anything. She also had a car, so she could take me anywhere I wanted.

On one occasion, I encountered a group of teenagers mocking me, commenting on my appearance and backpack at a metro station. Although I initially brushed it off, their behavior escalated when one of them tugged at the string on my backpack as I stood on an escalator. My anger was palpable, but I was unsure how to react. It was then I confided in Beth. Her reaction was fierce, angry at the teens for their behavior and empathetic toward my experience. She assured me that most Americans treat people with kindness and respect, encouraging me to assert myself if a similar situation arose. From that day on, Beth always asked me about my metro ride. She also showed a pepper spray she carried in her purse and suggested I carry one too.

She was kind to everyone in the office, especially to me and Sylvia, a Latino woman, because we were new to the country.

As a white woman, she had no special pride. Her warmth created an environment of equality, erasing any sense of difference. Our lunchtime and after-work chats formed a cherished routine. These interactions and Beth's infectious smile brightened my days, making me look forward to Mondays. Her humility shone through as she sought to learn from me, boosting my confidence. She asked for my help with the mail merging function in Microsoft Word and Excel. She learned it quickly and thanked me for being patient with her. That boosted my confidence.

Beyond work, Beth's curiosity about China and my upbringing fostered meaningful conversations. She expressed her fondness for Chinese cuisine and her aspiration to explore its beauty. We also discussed girls' education, where I assured her of the strides made in major cities while highlighting rural disparities. Our exchanges went beyond work, bridging gaps and broadening perspectives.

During our conversations, I mentioned the challenging path to attending a good college in China due to the rigorous entrance exams. Although a reputable college accepted me, it wasn't the most prestigious one. Her response caught me off guard: "Lucy, you are smart. You are successful. You will be even more successful." Her unwavering confidence in me, despite our short acquaintance, was truly heartening.

At that juncture, I received an acceptance from UCLA, having previously been declined by the University of British Columbia. The anticipation of a scholarship from UCLA kept me on edge. When I finally shared the scholarship news with Beth, her excitement was palpable. She insisted on celebrating the achievement. She took me to Gifford's Ice Cream parlor, where I indulged in the most delightful ice cream. There, I experienced my first banana split, a memory I will forever associate with Beth's generosity and encouragement.

Besides taking me to the ice cream parlor, Beth taught me to play card games like gin rummy. Occasionally, she and I would play for half an hour after work. She reciprocated by sharing her own life story with me. As a single mother, she raised four children after her divorce. Her determination allowed her to support her children through their college education, and they all excelled in their respective fields. The most touching aspect was her deep love and close bond with each of them.

Days flew by very quickly. After spending a year and three months at the nonprofit organization, the moment came for me to bid farewell and transition to UCLA. Leaving Beth was not easy. In a heartfelt gesture, she took me to Outback, one of her favorite restaurants, for a farewell dinner. During our conversation, she continued to uplift me, reinforcing my strengths and capabilities and describing me as intelligent and resilient. She said to me, "I cannot wait to celebrate your graduation at UCLA!" The confidence she instilled in me carried over into my year of hard study.

GREEN CARD

In 1996, I embarked on my professional journey after graduating in the summer. I secured a position as an environmental engineer at an environmental consulting firm in Buffalo, New York. For an immigrant like me, obtaining a green card carried immense significance. I vividly recall the moment of panic when I realized I had misplaced one of the crucial visa documents. The sense of dread was overwhelming, and desperation set in. From the time I applied for my green card to finally receiving it, two years of waiting, checking, and hoping passed. Compared to some of my friends who waited for five years or even longer, I was fortunate. This waiting period translated into limited job mobility, hesitance in salary negotiations, and the inability to easily relocate closer to my family. Basic liberties that native-born Americans took for granted were not readily accessible to immigrants like me.

Even after I got my green card, my sense of insecurity never completely vanished. My sense of food insecurity continued to linger, given the scarce resources I had growing up. Even now, I still have the habit of storing food. When traveling, the first thing I search for is food. I always make sure there's a food court near my hotel, and I carry snacks in my bags all the time. I guess subconsciously, I feel safer knowing food is readily available. Some say even a person such as Angela Merkel, the German chancellor who grew up in East Germany, retains her early habits of food stockpiling (Connolly 2010).

FIRST PROFESSIONAL JOB
In the spring of 1997, I worked on an investigation project related to a household contamination incident in New Orleans. It excited me to work along with the contractors on the field. Among the crew members, a man made jokes about my accent from the very first day. Initially, I dismissed it, attributing it to the supposed American sense of humor. I also aimed to fit in and have others like me, not wanting to come across as overly sensitive.

However, as the days passed, the jokes escalated, and my embarrassment over my accent and language limitations grew. By the third day, frustration was mounting. On the fifth day, I asked him for a piece of duct tape, which we needed to seal the sleeves of our personal protection suits. His response hit me like a blow: "I'm not going to marry you."

At that moment, my smile froze, and I felt a surge of emotions—shame, anger, and sadness. I walked away, my mind spinning with confusion. Later that night, tears flowed freely.

After discussing the incident with a friend, I mustered the courage to report it to my project manager. The following morning, the man apologized to me over the phone. Later in the day, management dismissed him from his position. While a sense of justice prevailed, I couldn't help but feel a pang of empathy for him. I wished there had been a better resolution, one where understanding could have prevailed over a layoff. While I hoped he had learned a valuable lesson, I, too, gained insights from this experience. Years later, I realized I should have spoken up earlier, right from the beginning, if I ever felt upset or uncomfortable. It was a lesson in asserting my feelings, handling confrontations, and establishing clear boundaries in the workplace. At that particular time, I lacked the knowledge of how to effectively articulate my emotions.

In addition to the job insecurity challenges, I also faced loneliness. Upon moving to Buffalo, New York, in 1996 to begin my first job, I found myself without any friends in the area. Those initial two winters were especially tough. The harsh weather, a far cry from the mild climate of Los Angeles, where I pursued my graduate studies, was a significant adjustment. I had to learn how to navigate snowy roads, defrost windshields, and prepare supplies before venturing out.

Those were particularly challenging days, especially in the aftermath of ending a long-term relationship. Tears often accompanied my nights, and in the morning, I would put on makeup to disguise my swollen eyes. I refrained from sharing too much with my parents, just as I did during my childhood, for fear of adding to their worries. They had already done so much for me, and I didn't want to burden them further. I recall my habit of walking along the shores of Lake Erie after work. I would let the wind whip against my face, almost as if it were an external manifestation of the whirlwind within me.

There was a day when I stood by the dark expanse of the lake, and an unsettling thought crossed my mind: What if I were to fall into the water and drown? No one would notice me. No one would have known it for a long time. Sometime later, my parents would have to report me missing to the police, and they would find my body in the lake—or not. My parents would cry hard and never be able to recover from losing me. This brief, stark moment shook me to my core. Swiftly, I wiped away my tears and resolved within myself. I couldn't allow such a notion to gain ground. I reminded myself I needed to survive and muster the strength within me. It was a fleeting thought, yet it spurred me to embrace life with renewed determination.

Despite the engulfing loneliness in Buffalo, a glimmer of brightness persisted. A close friend from my college years in Cincinnati invited me to spend Thanksgiving with her. Her homemade steamed buns surpassed restaurant fare, and her kind words provided solace. I also cultivated meaningful friendships at work, particularly among my fellow Chinese colleagues. Inviting me into their homes, they treated me to traditional Chinese meals and celebrated Chinese New Year together, easing my yearning for the past. The move of one of my closest friends from China to Toronto brought additional joy. Her warm invitation to visit her and her husband served as a safe space for me to share my work frustrations and personal struggles. Their patient listening and words of encouragement provided a steady beacon of hope. The relocation of my brother and sister-in-law to Toronto in 1997 was serendipitous. Bi-weekly visits, driving two hours each way, allowed me to find respite and connection within the embrace of family. The convergence of friendship and family provided much-needed support during my darkest hours. By the onset of spring in 1998, I felt revitalized.

Determined to combat my isolation-induced weakness, I delved into exercise. Winter's perfect pursuit, ice skating, became a weekly endeavor. A dance class introduced me to ballet and swing, adding zest to my routine. Swimming, too, became a regular fixture. These activities invigorated my body and mind. Joining a Chinese choir further facilitated connections with others, offering weekly engagement. A friend began inviting me to a nearby church, granting me my first opportunity of exposure to Christianity.

Above all, a rekindled connection marked a turning point. An old Chinese friend from my UCLA days reentered my life. By the summer of 1998, our shared history and mutual interests led to a profound decision—marriage. This fresh chapter epitomized the emergence of hope and love in my life.

RELOCATION TO SAN FRANCISCO

During this period, he resided in LA, embarking on the final stages of his PhD. As our relationship deepened, I recognized that sustaining a long-distance connection would be a challenge. I was determined to move closer to him. However, I could not switch to a new job because I was in the middle of my green card application, which was through a sponsorship by my company. The only viable path was to persuade my company to relocate me to a location closer to my partner. Although I knew our firm had offices in Los Angeles and San Francisco, I grappled with uncertainty regarding their willingness to accommodate my request.

Summoning my courage, I formulated a plan, although it meant stepping far beyond my comfort zone and embracing considerable risk. What if the senior management did not share my vision and even deemed me not worth keeping? The economy was relatively weak, heightening the risk. My strategy hinged on bypassing my immediate manager and engaging with our CEO directly. If he endorsed my proposal, I could navigate the path ahead more smoothly. If he rejected it, I had a contingency plan to appeal through my manager and other channels. Our successful collaboration informed this decision on a recent project, which fostered a degree of familiarity and recognition from the CEO.

One afternoon, around 5:30 p.m., I took the courage to knock on his door. At that time, most of my colleagues had gone home. I waited for the right moment the entire day. I practiced my pitch over and over again until I knew my lines very well. My heart thumped so hard. Engaging in casual conversation, I then broached the topic that had been on my mind all day.

I asked if I could relocate to either Los Angeles or San Francisco while retaining my current role. The reason was simple: I intended to build a life with my fiancé and committed myself to maintaining my diligent work ethic. He listened attentively, nodding as I outlined my proposal. In a heartbeat, he granted his approval. Joy surged within me. While I refrained from outward celebration in his presence, inwardly, I was leaping and dancing with elation. The chosen destination was San Francisco due to project requirements. Though it wasn't my preferred location of LA, it wasn't too far either.

Swiftly, I conveyed the news to the HR director and my immediate manager. Their happiness mirrored my own. While reflecting, I realized I could have perhaps negotiated for a raise, given the high cost of living in the San Francisco Bay Area, particularly in Silicon Valley. Yet, this notion didn't cross my mind initially. I was content with the outcome and, in my view, requesting a raise might have come across as greedy or ungrateful.

Every step fell into place seamlessly, from concluding my lease and packing up to the actual move itself. I was fortunate to have the unwavering support of my friends in Buffalo and Toronto, who stood by me throughout the process. Within two months, I successfully transitioned to the San Francisco Bay Area. The year 1999 saw me not only relocating to this new chapter of my life but also entering into marriage. The loneliness that once gripped me has become a distant memory. God answered my heartfelt prayers, and for that, I hold a profound sense of gratitude.

CHAPTER 4

MY AGING PARENTS

A joyful heart is good medicine.
—PROVERBS 17:22

Following their retirement, Dad and Mom chose to live near me, living a life of modesty and simplicity like before. After becoming a Christian in his seventies, Dad followed Jesus's example, actively aiming to be humble and gentle. He dedicated himself to studying the Bible and engaging in daily prayers, extending his care and compassion to the brothers and sisters around him. His retirement life was full of joy and laughter, and he attributed everything to the grace of God.

ALZHEIMER'S

My parents' journey with dementia began several years ago, or rather—that's when I first noticed the signs. It started with minor incidents like them getting locked out of their apartment and needing my assistance. Then, I began to spot tiny fruit flies swarming around the kitchen, particularly near the decaying apples on the counter. Their confusion between the refrigerator and closet led them to store food in unexpected places, which produced rotten smells and more fruit flies. They were apologetic each time I discovered the situation. Over time, they forgot to take medications and pay rent. The once-familiar gadgets like their iPad and cell phones turned into confusing tools. Gradually, the ability to operate even simple appliances like the toaster and microwave, as well as the fundamental task of locking and unlocking doors, vanished. Their living space descended into a mess.

They had lost so much weight because of skipped meals. Remarkably, they expressed concern for me, feeling remorseful that the extensive care I provided consumed my time—cleaning up their rooms, arranging their clothes, cooking for them, and reminding them about their medication.

Between them, Mom's battle with dementia was more challenging. I experienced immense frustration at the outset because the once-strong, intelligent, and vibrant individuals they were seemingly faded away. Both had excelled in physics, displaying intelligence, unwavering determination, and remarkable resilience. They had been a source of towering inspiration in my view. How could I forget the times when Dad took my brother and me on bike rides to the Beijing Zoo, carrying us on his shoulders and climbing the stairs to our apartment unit after an entire day of hiking and playing? He was the embodiment of strength. Where was that father who could seemingly conquer the world? And what about the mother who effortlessly tackled the most intricate physics and math problems and crafted the most beautiful red skirt for me?

Recognizing the urgency and determined to assist them, my priorities were clear: ensuring their meals and medications, maintaining cleanliness, and fostering social interaction. However, convincing them of the need for external assistance was a challenge. No matter my gentle or assertive approach, I struggled to make them understand. They refused any outside help.

Yet, I found a creative solution. I arranged for the caregiver to prepare the meals at my home first and then called my parents to receive the meals downstairs, claiming they were leftovers from the restaurant. Eventually, I convinced them the caregiver needed to prepare food at their apartment.

To maintain cleanliness, I adopted a different approach. Initially, I entered with the cleaning woman, and together we tackled the cleaning tasks. The following week, I informed my parents that a business meeting had kept me away, leaving the cleaning woman to complete the work alone. Gradually, they became accustomed to her regular visits. As time passed and their self-sufficiency declined, I extended the caregiving hours and frequency. The COVID-19 pandemic dealt a severe blow to my parents' situation. Due to safety concerns, I had to reduce the number of caregivers, leading to heightened isolation and worsening dementia. To counterbalance this, I arranged for my older daughters to take turns spending two hours a day with their grandparents. This increased their interaction with the outside world and strengthened a special bond between the generations.

At the beginning of 2020, my parents struggled to recall my daughters' names, even though we gathered as a family every week. However, by the summer of that year, they had grown fond of my daughters' company and could remember their names. Their phone conversations sounded amusing, even though I could only hear my daughter's side of the phone conversation.

"Grandma, do you know how old I am?"

"Close, but I'm not twelve. I'm twenty."

"Grandpa, do you know my mom's name?"

"No, my mom's name is not Min. It's Lucy."

"Grandma, how old are you?"

"Almost correct. You are not sixty. You are eighty-two."

One day, my eldest daughter recounted an interaction with her grandma.

"Grandma got really excited and started talking about the Tangshan earthquake and how we had to escape…"

It dawned on my daughter that Grandma was referring to me, not her because that was 1976. It was a bittersweet moment, highlighting my mom's confusion. A sense of worry crept in. Would Mom remember me? This reminded me of Eric Clapton's famous song, "Tears in Heaven." He wrote the song when coping with the sudden death of his four-year-old son and wondered if his son would recognize him in heaven. In 2020, I contemplated the song's theme, unsure if my parents would remember me one day, whether in heaven or on this earth.

DAD'S FINAL DAYS

Tragically, on top of Alzheimer's, Dad received a Parkinson's diagnosis in his seventies. Throughout the years, I witnessed his transition from relying on a cane to a walker and eventually to a wheelchair. Dad's Parkinson's disease worsened after his eightieth birthday. This neurological condition has no known cause or cure. Nevertheless, my parents believed mercury poisoning from his youth might have been the cause. Over time, Dad became increasingly inactive, moved slowly, and spoke less. For a period, I grappled with the reality that they had transformed into individuals who required care and exhibited childlike behavior.

One of the most heartrending moments was witnessing Dad walk trembling with his walker and his shoulders tilted to balance along each step. He was so fragile that even a breeze might knock him down. Nonetheless, during his final years, he fought his illness tenaciously until the very last moment. The pain incapacitated him as a former sportsman and an outstanding speaker as he lost his verbal skills. Yet, neither defeated his will as he faced everything with joy and redefined strength and resilience.

Although he lived an abundant life, his health deteriorated dramatically before his passing in 2021–2022. Unfortunately, Dad had already gone into a coma before he passed away, but I still made sure to whisper good news to him about my daughters at his bedside: "The grace of the Lord Jesus baptized BaoBao and BeiBei today! Thank you for your prayers!" I believe he could hear this happy news. While I often perceived myself as inexperienced and simple, in his view, I remained a pearl of purity and beauty, held securely within his caring palm.

In the end, he was a blessed man surrounded by a loving family and friends. Just like my eldest daughter stated in her eulogy at his funeral, "I learned from *Grandpa* to not dwell on the inevitable end. Why dwell on the injustice of an incurable disease when you can celebrate having loved ones join in the fight? He has often overcome the possibility of death—through war, revolution, and sickness—and doesn't this further prove how blessed he truly was? It is a blessing he refused to let adversity harden him. He made a better life for my mother and me through his sacrifices. He instilled in me a love for art and for the piano. When I played the piano for him, I was living his dream."

MOM'S DEMENTIA

"What's your father's name?" I heard Mom softly inquire. "My father's name is Liuzhu. His family name is Li," her voice carried a sense of distant repetition. These were the same conversations she repeated again and again. Sometimes, they came once a week, and sometimes, they returned multiple times within a single day. Initially, I attempted to gently correct her by saying, "Mom, my grandpa's name was not Liuzhu." She would smile at me, acknowledging her mistake. However, mere moments later, she would repeat her own version of her father's name. Then, it struck me one day—the translation of *Liuzhu* is *to keep* in Chinese 留住. A wave of poignant sadness washed over me. It became clear that perhaps, from her early years, she held an unspoken wish to keep her father by her side, as if he had never left her.

These self-conversations began about a year ago, following Dad's passing. Over the past decade, she had tirelessly cared for my father until his passing in 2022. Strangely, it seems Mom has forgotten Dad just a few days after his departure. It was almost inconceivable to see how she had entirely erased the man who adored her for an incredible fifty-six years. She no longer mentions Dad's name; the memory of the handsome man seated beside her in their engagement photograph has evaporated.

I visit her every day, even if it's just for a few moments, hoping she will remember me.

"What a surprise to see you, my daughter! Long time no see!" My mom greets me with a smile whenever I visit her.

"Look, dumplings. It's Chinese New Year's Day! How wonderful." Just like when I was little, she moved her own dishes in front of me, inviting me to eat the delicious food. I felt sad watching her childlike innocence; every day is Chinese New Year's Day in her eyes.

She spends most of her days being joyful as her caregiver accompanies her on outdoor walks, senior activities, and church visits. I take over caregiving duties on Saturdays not only to give her caregiver a break but also so she will not forget me. However, a change occurred after the Chinese New Year of 2023. She began engaging in negative self-talk, imagining someone scolding or hitting her, and crying for humiliation and shame. Initially, we could reassure her that she was safe and these events had not happened. Gradually, it became a struggle to break through her imaginary world. Even when she was watching joyful singing and dancing on TV, she sank into her dark world of sadness. She persisted in mumbling these terrible thoughts and shedding tears, which deeply saddened us. We tried various methods to distract her from this emotional drain and danger, but we failed, and it was heartache to find her wrapped in bitterness.

I reached out to her doctor and got confirmation that this was a natural part of the dementia process. I lost sleep because I was eager to seek ways to pull her out of this vicious cycle. I did not want to give up hope. Then, one day, I overheard her caregiver reciting children's songs and encouraging Mom to join her. Mom smiled and attempted to follow. Though she had difficulty repeating the whole song, her caregiver patiently guided her. This sparked an idea within me.

I began teaching Mom several children's poems and songs I learned when I was little. I taught my children these when they were little. Whenever Mom started murmuring negative thoughts, I would gently interrupt and invite her to recite children's songs. Day by day, a change occurred. Mom started to improve. She smiled when she recited these songs even though the tears on her face had not dried.

I discovered a new way to break through her negative thoughts whenever she mentioned someone yelled at her or hit her. I would swiftly suggest replacing those words with *praise* to make it positive. For instance, if she said, "Mao scolded me last night." I would suggest, "How about changing *scold* to *praise*?" Her response would be, "Mao praised me last night." I would clap my hands and praise her, "Great job, Mom!" Over time, this game became familiar to her, and she began using positive words more frequently than negative ones. It changed her mood from an unhappy to a happy one. What a relief it was to see her smile again!

Mom's mind transformed, just like a little child's. I hope that negative words will eventually disappear from her imaginary world and vocabulary, given all her numerous hardships in life. Why not let her spend happy moments in her final days? Through this journey, I have learned to be loving, patient, and sympathetic with her.

COVID-19 AND RECENT INCIDENTS

Over the past three years, I became extremely protective of my parents' safety concerning COVID-19 exposure. With the pandemic officially declared over at the beginning of 2023 and people around us resuming travel, and after Mom received several rounds of vaccination, I thought we were finally in the clear and wouldn't have to worry about getting COVID-19. In the summer of 2023, I took Mom on a seven-day trip to Alaska, hoping the change of scenery would stimulate her mind. However, life had other plans for us.

Four days after returning from her trip, Mom contracted COVID-19 and tested positive. It was a typical Friday afternoon; it always seems like urgent things happen right before the end of the week or over the weekend. I had to wait to secure an online appointment with her doctor and finally got the prescription for Paxlovid, the drug to treat COVID-19. That night, Mom took the first dose. Thankfully, she began to look better on Sunday. Then, it was my turn to feel exhausted and sick and start coughing as I tested positive for COVID-19 too. While having a high fever myself, I continued to take care of Mom through the weekend. Fortunately, by Monday afternoon, both Mom and I felt better.

Just when I thought things were settling down, another incident occurred that left me shaken. While washing dishes in her kitchen, I heard Mom scream, followed by a loud thump in the living room.

Rushing to her aid, I found her lying on the floor and crying, "My head hurts so much!" She was trying to reach the back of her head.

Her head bumped on the side of the dining table when she fell.

While comforting her, "There, there. That's okay. No worries." I used one hand to massage her back head and the other hand to help her get up.

I was panicking but trying to remain calm. Suddenly, I noticed my hand that touched Mom's head was full of blood, and more blood streamed down to her neck. For a split second, my mind went blank, and I acted on instinct, mechanically grabbing napkins to wipe away the blood. But it kept gushing out, soaking the first napkin and the second, and panic started to set in.

"Oh, my goodness! What am I going to do?" I could not think properly, overwhelmed by the scene.

Taking a deep breath, I paused, wondering if I should call 9-1-1.

But the memory of Dad's experience, confined in rehab and under strict quarantine rules in December 2021, rushed into my mind. I couldn't bear the thought of Mom going through the same ordeal. With her dementia, being isolated in a rehab facility without us at her side would pose a serious danger for her. She only recognizes me, my brother, and her caregivers, so if forced to stay in a strange environment without us, she could go insane and die... Taking another deep breath, I decided not to call 9-1-1 but rather to assess the situation.

As I observed Mom, I noticed she could breathe, speak, and recognize me: these were positive signs. I decided to stay calm and apply pressure to her wound for a couple of minutes first. I have been Mom's power of attorney given her dementia. This decision was one of the hardest decisions I've ever made because her life was in my hands. Thankfully, the bleeding eventually stopped. I carefully cut her hair around the wound area and found the wound was as small as a tiny button and appeared dry. What a relief! Two days later, I was glad to see a full recovery from both COVID-19 and her injury. Mom had totally forgotten about the incident, returning to a state of joyfulness and peacefulness.

Though COVID-19 has passed, her dementia persists. I tell myself there is no need to be sad about her memory loss as long as she is happy. It is her blessing to live in her little world and soak in her own joy. It is fine that she cannot remember her friends and family as long as she feels love. I will continue the journey of taking care of Mom, the journey of not necessarily helping her to recover but slowing down the loss of her memory of her loved ones.

I will continue with unwavering resilience.

PART II

SEVEN PRINCIPLES TO BUILD RESILIENCE

CHAPTER 5

PRINCIPLE 1: NURTURING AND HEALING

———

Resilience is knowing that you are the only one that has
the power and the responsibility to pick yourself up.
—MARY HOLLOWAY

One valuable life lesson instilled in me by my parents is the belief that I am resilient and I can conquer anything if I set my mind to it. They also taught me that through self-care, self-compassion, and nurturing the power that lies within, I can cultivate resilience.

It was two months before my college entrance exam in 1988. I felt incredibly stressed, but I knew I had to summon my strengths to study hard and dash to the finish line. The college entrance exam in China is the world's toughest school exam because of its notoriously difficult questions (e.g., the level of some math questions in the college entrance exam is comparable to university-level math in the UK.) Arguably, this one exam determines a student's fate—the college one attends as well as career and other aspects of life (Ash 2016).

"Take a nap. You will recharge," Mom reminded me while touching my forehead to ensure I did not have a fever.

"I cannot. I have no time and a lot to study," I declined her suggestion.

"Your health comes first, my daughter. You are too stressed out. Relax and you will be fine." She replied, adding, "Tension will weaken your body. You will perform better if relaxed and confident."

I was sick for five months on and off that year, with a sore throat, coughing, and headache. I could feel my body sending signals of exhaustion, urging me to take a nap to restore my mind and energy. Little did I realize, at the time, that there was a direct link between my illness and the stress I put on myself—scores, expectations, and the future. Fortunately for me, my mom was there with a wise and gentle reminder of the importance of self-care. Those naps wound up helping me tremendously in my recovery process.

After the entrance exams, as the stress subsided for every student, I restored my health and reflected on some lessons I learned through the experience. First, I began to understand the harm of chronic stress to my health. Second, during the final stage of preparation, managing stress is even more critical than studying itself because personal well-being should be a priority. Third, those who effectively manage stress can be some of the most resilient individuals because they perform better while maintaining well-being.

I've discovered you acquire resilience through self-nurturance and healing as you tap into your inner strengths.

FACTS ABOUT NURTURING AND HEALING

OUR RESILIENT BUILT-IN SYSTEM

In *Man's Search for Meaning*, Viktor Frankl, a survivor of the Jewish concentration camp as well as a neurologist and psychologist, mentions remarkable human abilities. He describes the unimaginably harsh environment in the Auschwitz camp during WWII. While many perished, he was surprised by the resilience that some displayed.

He states, "I would like to mention a few similar surprises on how much we endure: we were unable to clean our teeth, and yet, in spite of that and a severe vitamin deficiency, we had healthier gums than ever before" (Frankl 1946). He recalls they wore the same shirts for half a year until they were unrecognizable and limited water access. Yet, despite the harsh and dirty environment, they had no infections from sores. In addition, a slight sleeper began to be able to fall asleep even when sleeping close to a comrade who snored loudly. As a trained medical doctor, he was particularly astonished by the survival abilities of the human body. Even though the book does not mention the word resilience, he teaches readers that survival relies on resilience related to his cultivation of mind and finding purpose. For him, it was to reunite with his family, publish his book, and continue his teaching.

I'm not implying that our human bodies can withstand prolonged exposure to harsh conditions. Rather, my perspective centers on our inherent capacity to endure and recuperate from adversities, whether they be trauma, illness, or other challenges. No matter how much our doctors do for us, what helps us heal is our own immune system, which has more self-healing capacities than we imagine.

More importantly, we need to believe in the powers within us to strengthen ourselves. This belief shields us from succumbing to a victim mentality when confronted with challenges.

THE MIND-BODY CONNECTION

According to Anne Harrington, a professor at Harvard University and author of *The Cure Within: A History of Mind-Body Medicine*, the popularity of mind-body medicine has stemmed from dissatisfaction with mainstream medicine in recent years (Harrington 2008). Hippocrates's quote, "The natural healing force within each one of us is the greatest force in getting well," encapsulates this concept. Similarly, Mount Sinai Hospital defines mind-body medicine as using thoughts and emotions to impact physical health while highlighting how negative emotions can impair healing and health. Few realize just how emotions can affect overall health and well-being (Icahn School of Medicine at Mount Sinai 2023).

In turn, others have addressed the placebo effect, emphasizing that the mind can indeed heal the body. In her TEDx

Talk, "Is there scientific proof we can heal ourselves?" Lissa Rankin emphasizes that the mind can heal the body. She cites the placebo effect and spontaneous remission cases from the Spontaneous Remission Project (Rankin 2012). The placebo effect is an improved effect produced by an inactive drug or treatment due to the patient's belief in that treatment (Wahbeh 2023).

Rankin shared the story of Mr. Wright, who battled advanced lymphosarcoma in 1957. With tumors the size of oranges in various body parts, he pleaded with Dr. West for Krebiozen, a wonder drug. After three days, his tumors shrank by half, and in ten days, they vanished completely. Wright enjoyed two months of health and joy, fueled by faith in the drug. Yet, depression struck when he learned the drug's effectiveness wasn't as doctors reported. Dr. West then claimed the initial drug was impure and administered distilled water. Tumors disappeared again, and he felt well for two more months. However, despair returned upon news that the American Medical Association discredited Krebiozen. Devastated, Wright passed away two days later. This saga illustrates the mind's potent impact on the body's healing processes.

Similarly, Rankin observes that there is scientific proof of the mind helping the body heal, with physiological measurements reinforcing the evidence. Here, she mentions that Dr. Ted Kaptchuk, a Harvard researcher, affirmed the quality of care under the physicians, pointing out that the physicians were in fact the placebo. Even though the doctor disclosed to the patients he was giving them a placebo with no effect, the patients still got better—because they felt tended, nurtured, and cared for.

In other words, the mind has considerable influence on our bodies. That's why understanding the mind-body connection empowers us to cultivate mental strength, ultimately enhancing our ability to overcome adversity and maintain overall health.

THE MIRACLE OF HEALING

Now, let's turn to a powerful testimony from Dr. David Reilly.

Reilly, a former consultant physician and the director of TheWEL Programmes and The Healing Shift Enquiry in Glasgow, Scotland, builds his work on his foundational observations that Life has an innate strength—a drive toward healing and wholeness and Life responds to nurture. He uses a capital L here to distinguish the Life, the aliveness, in us from our ever-changing life situations. Based on thirty years of research and clinical results, his work centers upon the activation of self-sustaining self-care, which in turn taps the well of our innate strengths for healing, health, and happiness.

His TEDx Talk, "Human Healing Unlocked: transforming suffering into wellbeing," explored these themes of working with our innate strengths (Reilly 2017).

In 1984, a nineteen-year-old named Andrea consulted with Reilly because of a nonfunctioning bladder she suffered from the age of seven. As she contemplated having her bladder removed, she set a date for the surgical removal of her bladder and had been referred to him as a last resort. Reilly listened deeply to her story during the first session. That night, Andrea had a dream about an old memory. She told him she had recalled a man who had looked through the window of her bathroom from the street when she was seven and felt this must have been the cause of her bladder dysfunction. She thought this insight might heal her. After months of no progress, she returned to see Reilly again. He recommended hypnosis, but she refused. That brought Reilly to a halt for a moment, concerned he might be unable to help her. But he did not give up—he asked if she ever daydreamed. When she answered, "Yes, all the time," Reilly invited her to daydream with him. He gave her enough space to review the past trauma and express her emotions comfortably before gently offering different ways to view the situation. After the session, she initially got much worse as she lost the capacity to urinate over a twelve-hour span. Then, something remarkable happened—appearing healed completely, she remained so at least through 2017 when the TEDx Talk took place. The therapy session with Reilly allowed her mind to shift its perception of the past, and the resultant profound inner shifts restored her body's original functions.

Reilly's TEDx Talk fascinated me because of his point of view, theory, and stories. Fortunately, I had an opportunity to interview him about his research and evidence. Reilly shared more of his research program, and findings focused on patients with chronic suffering, illness, and loss of well-being.

I asked Reilly how we can nurture ourselves when facing challenges. He used the metaphor of a plant to describe Life. He said, "If you see a plant struggling from lack of water—what do you feel? There is an action impulse—we want to bring it water. This happens when our compassion toward Life opens— like the response of a mother to a child or the owner to a pet.

This unlocks what I call the nurture response. You have a fight-or-flight response, but we also have a nurture response. Activate that toward life, and change becomes unstoppable."

In facing life's challenges, we must care for and cultivate ourselves like a gardener tending to a delicate plant. It goes beyond the notion of merely *toughing it out*. It's about believing in ourselves, nurturing our bodies and spirits, and allowing ourselves to build resilience, which starts with self-confidence and self-care.

NURTURE THE BODY AND MIND

Both Dr. Rankin and Dr. Reilly validated that humans have the built-in ability to restore our bodily functions with nurturing and healing. This powerful ability may help us overcome life's physical or mental challenges.

Remember the incredible healing power of my dad's special nutrition recipe, the tomato pork bone soup he concocted to fight his tuberculosis? His soup was the placebo that helped him heal from TB, a disease widely regarded as incurable. During a time of scarce resources, the soup was probably the most nutritious food he could make for himself. Within just three months, his TB completely healed, astounding his doctor, who had never witnessed such a rapid recovery. Beyond his focus on nurturing his body with optimal nourishment, another pivotal element driving this rapid recovery was his resolute belief in his body's intrinsic capacity to heal itself. His sustained confidence played an instrumental role in catalyzing his physical healing process. In the face of adversity, his positive mindset became his guiding star in the fight against disease, reinforcing the profound connection between mind and body.

My mother was no less determined to thrive. Growing up as an orphan during wartime, she faced malnutrition, leading to a thin and short stature. Yet, these challenges couldn't dim her unyielding belief in her own strength. Over the years, she learned to take good care of her physical well-being and developed her own way to uphold a positive attitude and embrace optimism. She would sing joyfully, talk to flowers when no one was around, and firmly believe in her resilience. Deep in her heart, she believed her parents' wishes for her were to live a long and healthy life. In her words, she convinced herself, "Nothing can defeat me. My parents sacrificed their lives for me, and I will live." These positive practices and beliefs became a lifeline, guiding her through lonely nights and illness.

In addition to her personal efforts, her resilience blossomed under the nurturing care and support of others. Among these exceptional individuals, her aunt Dagu played a pivotal role. In fact, she credits Dagu for saving her life at a critical juncture. Hearing that her niece was ill, Dagu decided to visit her and stay for a few days to tend to her. My mother's fever dropped, and she could eat and drink. However, once her aunt departed for her own home, my mom's illness returned with the same severity. Feeling desperate and longing for her aunt's care, my mother wished for her aunt's return. The following week, when Dagu showed up, Mom's symptoms faded once again. This cycle continued for about two months. Finally, Dagu decided to stay longer until Mom fully recovered. My mom discovered something magical within her aunt's love and care. Dagu had told her she was strong and resilient and able to beat the disease in the end. Because she had no medical miracles or medicines involved, my mother's case reveals the sheer strength of her own will to live, strongly supported by her aunt's empathy and love, which brought the healing she needed. By nurturing Mom's body, soul, and mind, Dagu expedited the recovery process.

Although my mother and I are very different, we have several shared experiences. Like Mom, I was also fortunate enough to have a loving relative care for me—namely, my great-aunt, who took care of me during my childhood. One day, I pinched my finger when trying to bend a sugar stick, and blood gushed out. I ran back home to find my great-aunt. We had no bandages, antibacterial ointments, or other medicine. My great-aunt collected some dust from the wood door bolt and put it on my finger. This seemed to stop the bleeding, and my finger healed after a few days. As a six-year-old, I thought the dust had magic power, so I called it magic medicine. Eventually, of course, I learned the dust had no healing power. The dust was a placebo that healed me. My great-aunt's presence and caring boosted my confidence in my healing capability.

Over the years, I also learned to adopt Mom's determination. The first such instance was when I accidentally fractured my left arm bone at the age of eleven. My goal was crystal clear after the doctor removed the cast from my left arm. I must have a straight arm, the same as before. But it was too stiff to move, even just a tiny bit. The doctor advised me to spend thirty minutes doing a daily exercise of extending my arm bit by bit. It was initially hard because of the sheer pain, and my tears streamed down on the first day. I felt disappointed I did not see any progress at the end of the first day. Because of the excruciating pain, each time I tried to extend my arm, I spent five minutes extending it and rested for two minutes. I repeated it again and again until I was exhausted and sweated hard.

The following days were disappointing, too—but I did not give up. Progress finally appeared after one week of continuous effort as my arm could finally expand a tiny degree. Even though the change was insignificant, I could tell the difference. It was rewarding! Slowly, inch by inch, my arm could open more and more in the second and third weeks. I stuck firmly to the thirty-minute exercise schedule every day. Some days, I exercised five to ten minutes more to speed up. After a month or so, I restored it to its original mobility. Mom was very proud, and my doctor praised me for toughing it out.

During the restoration process, I learned two valuable lessons. First, I had faith I could restore my arm to its original state with consistent effort. This belief fueled my motivation and kept me focused on my goal. Second, my determination to succeed empowered me to continue pushing forward and never give up. When encountering life's difficulties, we must cultivate a positive mindset and attitude.

Later on, in 2007, I faced the daunting challenge of giving birth to my youngest child because of my two previous cesarean sections. My desire for a natural birth to deliver my new baby clashed with cautious medical advice and a sobering statistic—a 1.36 percent risk of uterine rupture during vaginal birth. Immediate medical intervention within a ten- to thirty-five-minute window was crucial in case of uterine rupture, which posed grave risks to both the baby and the mother.

However, against these odds and advice, my faith in my body's inherent capability remained steadfast. My quest for a well-informed choice led me to immerse myself in research and diverse perspectives. Encountering stories of successful natural childbirths reinforced my belief in navigating this path. Acknowledging that throughout history, women have birthed naturally without medical intervention, I remained resolute in my decision to pursue a natural birth. With unfaltering confidence in my body, I decided to pursue a natural birth. Because the medical odds were against me, I committed to rigorous preparation. I carefully balanced daily exercise, diet, and rest to nurture my physical and mental well-being.

To mitigate the risk of uterine rupture, I opted against any medications during labor, including induction and pain relief. This decision would minimize contraction pressure and intensity. In anticipation of potential complications, my medical team arranged for my transfer to a larger hospital, better equipped for surgical interventions. There, they suggested a precautionary measure—placing a spinal needle for immediate anesthesia delivery if surgery became necessary. This measure aimed to eliminate delays, ensuring swift administration of anesthesia through my spine if required. With preparations in place, I approached the unpredictable day of labor.

As the day of labor arrived, I faced hours of discomfort and pain, closely monitored by medical professionals as they tracked my baby's heartbeat for signs of distress. They presented the option of an epidural multiple times, yet I held fast to my decision. In moments of overwhelming pain, thoughts of resorting to medication briefly crossed my mind. However, I leaned on prayer and the Lamaze breathing technique, anchoring my energy in each breath and push while trusting in my body's resilience.

After a full fifteen hours of painful labor, including three hours of relentless pushing, I welcomed my daughter into the world without medication. Tears welled as her sweet fragrance enveloped the room, and a sense of relief, joy, and pride washed over me. This journey epitomizes the profound symbiosis between the determination of the mind and the capabilities of the body. By nurturing both elements, I defied the odds and showcased my strength within. In retrospect, my journey validated at least a few insights from Dr. Rankin's research while also echoing the sentiments of Dr. Reilly regarding the unlocking of human potential through the synergy of body and mind.

NURTURING MY SOUL

Nurturing can go beyond our physical health, extending to our souls. I can trace this lesson all the way back to the early days of childhood with my father, whose loving words taught me the importance of uplifting others with kindness and support. He would always shower me with praise, saying, "My daughter is the best!" I knew I could tell him anything without fearing a scolding.

Whenever Mom got mad at me, I would cry out, "Daddy, where are you?" wishing he could suddenly rescue me.

Indeed, traditional Chinese parenting prescribes a simple solution to children: be strict with them and always be ready to dish out tough love. Our culture believes that one must Ai Zhi Shen, Ze Zhi Qie 爱之深, 责之切— "love well, whip well." My father rejected that. He allowed me to freely express my thoughts and emotions. He permitted me to talk back to him and never took offense at my disrespectful comments. Instead, he just kept saying, "You are the best!" This is still rare in modern times—to say nothing of the past.

I didn't contemplate the reasoning behind my father's behavior until I became a parent, struggling with my strong-willed children during their adolescent years. I got mad whenever they argued with me, ignored my instructions, or challenged my authority. There were many times when I would feel overwhelmed and complain to my father, to which he would calmly answer with these simple words: "Love is patient. Love is kind." Just like with me, he never lost his temper or became disappointed with my children. There were also times when I feared I had punished them too harshly, but still, my father would comfort me by saying, "You are the best mom!" I simply could not understand him. Why was he always so kind to me?

I didn't find the answer until I watched Brené Brown's TEDx Talk, "The Power of Vulnerability" (Brown 2010). Her research reveals that feelings of shame and guilt stem from a person's belief he or she has flaws and, therefore, is unworthy of love and belonging. Simple as this may sound, we can better connect with others by helping them feel accepted—that they face no judgment and they are good enough. It was enlightening for me to discover that it strengthens people when simply given the power to say, "I am enough."

It was my father's way of nurturing me and helping me build my confidence. Whenever my father told me, "You are the best," I knew he meant that I had tried my hardest to be the best I could in my circumstances. So, today, I am the best version ever of Lucy Chen. He never said, "You are perfect." He trusted I was working hard to improve myself each and every day. That is all that any of us can do. Above all else, my father did his best to make me feel I am enough. I am good enough. I am strong enough. I am pretty enough. I am caring enough. I am intelligent enough. I am passionate enough. I am successful enough. I am enough!

This is why my father is my role model for parenting. The most important piece of parenting advice I ever got from him was this: Let your children know they are worthy of love and that they are enough. You cannot say it too many times. Looking back, the sense of confidence my father instilled within me has helped me survive many trials, including sickness, isolation, failure, and ultimately, his departure from this world. Though I stumbled in life countless times, I could always pick myself back up through the power of optimism—a belief my father taught me and I will always celebrate. He didn't confine his nurturing to the physical realm. It extended to nurturing my soul. In the same way that Dr. Reilly cared for his patients' well-being, my father's nurturing was a balm for my spirit, reinforcing my beliefs and enabling me to rise above life's tempests. Just as Dr. Reilly's patients received attentive care for their bodies, my father's approach encompassed the nurturing of my soul, unlocking my innate potential and resilience.

GUIDELINES
What we need to do is to practice self-care and adopt a positive mindset. For people around us, we need to understand their needs and provide a nurturing system to support them.

FIRST, PRACTICE MEDITATION AND MINDFULNESS

When we face life's challenges, our stress hormones increase dramatically. As part of the revolution, human beings respond to dangers with three actions—fight, flight, or freeze. The elevated hormones put our bodies into a highly reactive mode. Short-term stress saves us from life-threatening crises, but chronic stress can wreak havoc on our mind and body. Without a healthy mind and body, we cannot reach our life goals and live a successful life. That's why it's important to keep the first principle, nurturing and healing, in mind.

Meditation helps us to nurture and heal our body and mind. According to Mayo Clinic, "Meditation can give you a sense of calm, peace, and balance that can benefit both your emotional well-being and your overall health. You can also use it to relax and cope with stress by refocusing your attention on something calming. Meditation can help you learn to stay centered and keep inner peace" (Mayo Clinic Staff 2022).

According to *Neurotrition,* "Daily mindful meditation practice has been shown to produce measurable changes in brain regions associated with memory, sense of self, empathy, and stress. Studies have even documented changes in the brain's gray matter over time." Gray matter makes up 40 percent of brain matter. The structures within the gray matter process the signals involved in things like emotions, memory, speech, and muscle control. Practicing meditation nurtures our brain and improves its overall functioning (Mckinty 2023).

For people struggling with stress, meditation is one of the best practices of self-care. When I look inward around my belly or heart areas during the meditation, I feel peace, joy, love, and spaciousness. I feel I have enough energy and resources to overcome any obstacles in life. This positive emotion helps me develop confidence and builds hope for the future. Even for those not currently facing difficulties in life, practicing mindfulness brings focus, clarity, and peace of mind.

A daily practice of meditation, even for ten minutes, benefits our body, mind, and soul. It's an easy practice you can perform at home, in the office, or anywhere safe. My routine is to practice a guided meditation for fifteen minutes in the morning right after I wake up. It gives me a fresh start for a productive day.

Practicing mindful eating is another good habit. During the practice, I eat more slowly and chew the food thoroughly. I focus on how the food makes me feel and appreciate the sensation it brings to my mouth. During mindful eating, I feel gratitude toward food and life in general.

SECOND, SET UP A HEALTHY DAILY ROUTINE

Building resilience needs time and patience. If we can embed small steps into our daily routines, we may cultivate self-care, connect with our goals, and strengthen our resilience effectively. Healthy habits help us to actualize all seven principles. The following small steps go a long way.

1. Sleep

Dr. David Jockers, a natural medicine doctor specializing in functional nutrition and natural health strategies, reminds us that "Sleep is critical for every function of our body. Sleep is really when we heal. Sleep is when our brain detoxifies" (Jockers 2023). My friends always ask me the secret weapon of being energetic, young, and active—to which I answer, "a sound sleep of eight hours daily." I cannot stress enough the importance of a good night's sleep.

Our brain uses sleep as fuel, like food and water for our mind. During sleep, our brain builds and strengthens the neural connections that are the basis of our memory. However, when life gets hectic, the first thing that typically gets sacrificed is sleep. Sleep deprivation has become a worldwide epidemic.

Sleep nurtures our body and mind. It is the best way for our body to restore and enhance immune function. When we face life's challenges, our stress level tends to increase. Stress can prevent us from getting a reasonable amount of sleep; we have all experienced at one point or another the difficulty of falling asleep because of stress. Getting more sleep can significantly decrease cortisol levels and restore balance to the body's systems.

When I detect a higher stress level at the end of the day, I do meditation before sleep. Practicing meditation helps me to fall asleep faster. Using the breathing method of four-seven-eight helps me to remove stress. The method of four-seven-eight means you inhale for four counts, hold for seven counts, and exhale for eight counts. Another breathing method called box breathing, also known as four-square breathing, involves exhaling to a count of four, holding your lungs empty for a four-count, inhaling at the same pace, and holding air in your lungs for a count of four before exhaling and beginning the pattern anew. To maintain eight hours of sleep, I go to bed early. My regular sleep schedule starts at 10 p.m. and no later than 11 p.m. Also, I follow Chinese habits—taking a daily nap for fifteen minutes. Weekend naps are ideal for people who work at the office and have no place to nap during the day.

2. Morning

"Make your whole year's plan in the spring and the whole day's plan in the morning." My morning usually starts with thirty minutes of stretching, reading, meditation, and affirmation. My morning stretching activates my body's blood circulation and nourishes my body. Reading, even for five minutes, encourages creativity and imagination. The meditation keeps my mind calm, centered, and content. The daily affirmations boost my confidence and self-esteem.

In addition, I spend five minutes reviewing my daily planner and calendar. I usually perform my most important tasks in the morning. When I fully recharge after a good night's sleep, I have the energy to get things done efficiently in the morning. My stress is at the lowest level in the morning.

3. Affirmations

Our mind affects our body significantly. Positive thinking nurtures our body. Reciting daily affirmations nurtures our mind and reduces stress. My morning affirmations include the following simple sentences:

"I love myself."

"I control my life."

"I am grateful for life."

Another set of affirmations is useful for building my self-confidence:

"I am amazing."

"I am talented."

"I am beautiful."

"I am confident."

"I am successful."

"I am blessed."

These affirmations shift my mind from negative to positive thoughts. Positive thoughts give me the mindset to face any difficult situation and find solutions to solve problems.

4. Tune In with Our Inner Thoughts and Voices

Believing you can and you will is the starting point. Tuning in with our inner thoughts and voices allows us to nurture our mind and soul, even just five minutes. Our beliefs come from our inner world. We all live in our own virtual world—which is why we want to become our own guardians of our mind and emotion. Is this thought positive and nurturing? A positive and nurturing mind includes joy, peace, contentment, love, gratitude, etc. Negative and harmful mind and emotions include anger, frustration, loneliness, fear, etc. If we detect a negative emotion emerging, we need to ask ourselves what caused it. Then, we accept it and let it go.

I find the following practice I learned from the Human Potential Academy (https://humanpotentialacademy.io/) quite useful.

- Acknowledge your emotion, e.g., I am mad.

- Soften your eyes, soften your lips, soften your tongue, inhale and exhale slowly, and move your attention to your belly for one minute.

- Talk to yourself: I am feeling mad.

- Talk to yourself: I am aware I am feeling mad.

- Talk to yourself: I am aware, I am aware.

- Then open your eyes. During this practice called Gateway, you will no longer feel your emotions. Your body is like a conduit. Your emotion flows through your body and dissipates.

5. **Do Nothing Time for Ourselves**

We need to leave space for ourselves, even fifteen to twenty minutes a day. Our body and mind need time to be idle or alone time. It helps us to relax and rest. On busy days when my calendar has several meetings, I block half an hour for myself to *do nothing*.

6. Exercise

My dad was a proud member of his college's varsity basketball team and a fan of various sports—soccer, basketball, ping pong, and swimming. His love of physical activity was contagious, and he instilled in me the value of regular exercise as a fundamental aspect of self-care. He believed staying active kept our body fit and nurtured a strong and determined spirit. "Young people should exercise and sweat more," he explained. "It strengthens your body and your will to conquer challenges." While Mom was not as sporty as Dad, she also constantly reminded us to be active physically.

We need to stay active to improve our physical health and contribute to our mental and emotional resilience.

THIRD, PRACTICE SELF-CARE BASED ON CHINESE MEDICINE THEORIES

1. Hot Compress

Over the years, my father taught me how to use a warm towel absorbed with hot water to wrap body parts to speed up the healing. I learned this method from him. He used it to heal back pain, muscle pain, acne, boils, abscesses, as well as general discomfort in our body. In our family, we call it a *hot compress*. We called my dad the hot compress specialist. I have used this method countless times and taught my children how to do it too. It has become our family's secret healing method.

2. Pear Juice

We have a Chinese word *Shang Huo* 上火, meaning *excessive internal heat* or literally *on fire*. This is a concept in traditional Chinese medicine. People with excessive internal heat can easily get a sore throat, toothache, acne, inflammation, mouth ulcer, etc. That means your Yin and Yang, two opposing forces in your body, are out of balance. If someone is Shang Huo, they need to release and adjust the internal energy. One of the easy and simple methods is to eat *cooling* fruits such as pears.

When I had a sore throat or other Shang Huo symptoms, my mom would cut a pear into pieces and add water to boil these pieces, urging me to eat them. Sometimes, she added honey to the boiling mixture.

3. Massage Feet and Spine

We all know a massage improves circulation, stimulates muscles, and reduces tension. The foot contains meridians related to our internal organs, such as the spleen, liver, stomach, kidney, bladder, and gallbladder. Chinese medicine believes foot health is crucially important for the balance of the acupuncture energy system because all the body's acupuncture meridians either begin or end on the feet or hands. Chinese medicine also stresses that proper balance will support strong qi and vibrant health. Therefore, foot health is the foundation upon which whole body wellness rests (Pacific College of Health and Science 2023).

According to Dustin Martinez, a Los Angeles-based chiropractic physician, research shows that reflexology can improve quality of life in several ways. This involves reducing stress and bringing balance to the body, energy, and mind. "Reflexology is ancient medicine—it's been around forever," he says. "It can be traced as far back as 2330 BC" (Quinn 2022).

I learned from Mom to massage my feet whenever I got sick. My way is to soak feet in warm water for five minutes and then massage them for another five minutes. Doing it every day helps me improve my sleep quality and manage stress. It healed my period pain many years ago.

In addition, Mom also massaged and pinched the muscles along my spine when I was little. I'm not sure how much it helped me relieve the sickness and pains, but I definitely enjoyed the moments when her warm and affectionate hands touched my skin.

Humans can survive in a harsh environment, from healing from wounds, including mental trauma, to nurturing themselves and others. We have the innate strength and resources to cope with life hardships and bounce back from adversities. Practicing self-compassion will allow us to unlock our potential. It's important to believe we are resilient, to have an abundant life and overcome any difficulties. The key is to tap into our inner power. That requires us to develop healthy habits and daily routines. We need to follow our body's needs. Also, we need to create a nurturing environment for others, which will inevitably help them to unlock their potential.

CHAPTER 6

PRINCIPLE 2: GOALS, HOPES, AND DREAMS

———

*The future belongs to those who believe
in the beauty of their dreams.*
—ELEANOR ROOSEVELT

"What if they laugh at me?" A voice inside me piped up when I arrived at my daughter's high school baseball field. It was noon on March 23, 2022. I received an invitation to speak at the school's Diversity Week assembly on behalf of the Asian Pacific Islanders parents' engagement group. I felt nervous when the student representative extended her hand, welcoming me with a smile at the gate of the field. "Welcome, Ms. Chen!" Over one thousand students were walking in to get ready for the assembly.

I had spoken in front of hundreds of people in the audience, but they were all adults, and this was the first time I had ever given a speech in front of one thousand *teenagers*, along with teachers and school staff. I took a long and deep breath in and out at a slow pace. "No worries. I have done this kind of speech before. I can do it. Teenagers are people, people, people." My positive talk calmed me down. I straightened my shoulders, greeted the student, and followed her with my head held high to the podium where the panelists sat. During my speech, as I called for support and unity to stop Asian hate, many students widened their eyes and leaned forward, listening to my words. After wrapping up and hearing the loud applause from the audience, I handed the microphone to the next speaker, feeling very satisfied.

My dream of representing Asian Americans finally become a reality. Several years ago, the Asian American Rights Movement featured an inspiring quote from Jeremy Lin, a professional basketball player, "I want to be a representative and be a role model for the Asian American community" (Tabas 2023). It resonated deeply with me and has become my dream too—uplifting Asian Americans and raising our voices. Driven by his dreams, he became a role model for Asian Americans, excelling in basketball and using his platform to address racial stereotypes and biases in sports. Jeremy Lin's story stands as a testament to his remarkable resilience and unyielding determination.

Over the years, I have learned that having dreams, hopes, and goals during difficult times plays a crucial role in building resilience.

FACTS ABOUT GOALS, HOPES, AND DREAMS

Dr. Martin Luther King Jr.'s "I Have a Dream" speech is arguably the most famous reference to a dream. Delivered on August 28, 1963, the speech called for civil and economic rights and an end to racism in the US. It not only encapsulated the ideals of Dr. King but also of thousands of Blacks, people of color, and white Americans. He delivered the speech amid immense challenges and opposition. Despite facing violence and injustice, he urged people to persevere and not lose hope in the face of adversity. His speech called for immediate action to break racial barriers for all citizens with his vision for racial equality and his dream for a better future.

Dreams may not be as far-reaching as Dr. King's, but still serve a worthy, individual purpose in our lives. Humans are born with intrinsic values, and we are constantly searching for the means to validate our lives and values. As such, we develop hopes and establish goals for the future. These ambitions ignite our drive to venture into unknown territories, build meaningful relationships, and acquire new skills. More importantly, they serve as catalysts, pushing us forward to overcome obstacles that cross our paths. The article "On the Nature of Hope and Its Significance in Innovation," published by *Psychology Today*, emphasizes that hope is innate within us, ingrained in our DNA, and plays a pivotal role in turning dreams into reality (Ma 2014).

Hopes and dreams allow us to imagine a brighter future and envision a better life. According to Dr. Waters at the University of Melbourne and the author of *The Strength Switch,* hope pulls us into the future and, by doing so, helps us cope better with the present circumstances (Elkins 2023). Waters recommends using hope to cope with uncertainties or difficult situations since recent studies indicate that hope "leads us to maximize psychological adjustment by reducing anxiety, increasing motivation, and helping us pursue goal-directed actions."

According to positive psychologist Charles Richard "Rick" Snyder (1944–2006), hopeful thinkers achieve more and are physically and psychologically healthier than less hopeful people. He published six books about Hope Theory and 262 articles about the impact hope can have on aspects of life such as health, work, education, and personal meaning. Hope Theory argues that three main things make up hopeful thinking:

1. Goals: Approaching life in a goal-oriented way.

2. Pathways: Finding different ways to achieve your goals.

3. Agency: Believing you can instigate change and achieve these goals.

Snyder believes hopeful thinkers are people who can establish clear goals, imagine multiple workable pathways toward those goals, and persevere, even when obstacles get in their way (Mind Tools Content Team 2023).

The absence of hope for the future can leave us frustrated or even trapped in despair. People can also suffer mentally and physically because things look bleaker than they are in actuality. Too many negative thoughts can induce depression and anxiety. Even worse, people can become depressed or give up on life. At the same time, since our mind and body are more tightly conjoined than imagined, hopelessness can exacerbate physical issues. According to the *National Library of Medicine*, "There is compelling evidence pointing out that stress and depression produce a dramatic impact on human well-being mainly through impairing the regular function of the immune system and producing a low-chronic inflammation status that favors the occurrence of infections, metabolic diseases, and even cancer." (Cañas-González et al. 2020).

Viktor Frankl, a psychiatrist and the author of *Man's Search for Meaning*, mentioned a prisoner who had lost hope for his future, a fairly well-known composer and librettist (Frankl 1984). This fellow prisoner told Viktor one day he had a strange dream predicting the camp's liberation, and all their suffering ended on March 31, 1945. That conversation occurred in February 1945, only a month or so before the supposed day of liberation. He was full of optimism and pinned his entire hopes on this day. But the prisoner became desperate when the promised day drew near, and the war showed no signs of ending. On March 29, 1945, he suddenly fell ill and ran a high temperature. On March 31, 1945, the promised day, he died. To all, he died of typhus. But Viktor knew this man died of lost hope.

In the article "Viktor Frankl's Revelation of Hope," Steve Backlund suggests that Frankl, who helped millions embrace hope after his release from the concentration camps, held at the core of his therapy this truth: that human beings are driven by their views of their own future. The more positive the hope for the future, the more power and purpose there will be for the present (Backlund 2023). While imprisoned in a Nazi concentration camp, Frankl could endure intense suffering because he hoped to see his family again and write his book.

Backlund maintains that hope is the belief we have the power to make the future better than the present. "When we don't have this strong vision and purpose for the future, we will live from our past instead of our future. Our thinking will fixate on the past (regrets, good old days, if only, etc.), and, as a result, we will adopt a victim mindset and be without vitality in the present."

In *The Shawshank Redemption*, one of my favorite movies, the main character, Andy, spends nineteen years in prison for false accusations, enduring horrible physical and emotional struggles in prison. He does not give up hope and secretly chips away at his cell wall. When Andy and his friend Red are in prison, Red teaches Andy how to navigate the rotten prison and survive in the harsh and corrupted environment. But one thing Andy refuses is to give up his hope of living a free life with dignity. In the end, he is able to escape from the prison by going through the wall, connecting to the sewage tunnel and finding freedom. Andy helps Red to regain his hope back through his escape, encouragement, and friendship at the end of the movie.

PERSONAL EXPERIENCES

Mom strongly believed she would survive the wars and hardships as a young orphan because the hope of seeing her father sustained her for many years. Later on, when she realized it was impossible to see her father again, she imagined that staying alive and healthy would have been her parents' hope for her. Her existence was to actualize her parent's wish and her own wish to become a strong person.

Mom's experience in Sweden demonstrated the power of dreams and hopes in overcoming obstacles. Despite being forty-four years old and in a foreign country with a new language, her dream of creating new solutions in metal research motivated her to work tirelessly, spending countless nights alone in the lab with a determination to make a difference. Her hard work and dedication paid off, and two years later, she achieved remarkable accomplishments and received recognition for her innovation.

Dad was a visionary. While he resided in Sweden between 1978 and 1985, with the rest of the family in Beijing (Mom joined him in 1982), he crafted monthly letters addressed to each of us—Mom, my brother, and me. In these heartfelt letters, he not only recounted his experiences in this foreign land but also artfully depicted the picturesque moments of our future reunion. He invited us to dream with him, envisioning the exciting moments we would share, such as boating in parks and enjoying delicious meals together.

His words were so vivid I could easily visualize and dream with him. These letters not only helped him cope with the loneliness of being away but also eased our hearts, making us feel closer to him despite the distance. His letter taught me the importance of dreaming as a source of comfort during those long days and as a way to bond with loved ones regardless of the separation.

For Dad, the future always looked rosier because of dreams and hopes, even though his health deteriorated drastically before his passing. He cherished the vision of joyful family reunions with his grandchildren running around and enjoying food together; he longed to regain his strength and walk without the support of a walker. Not least did he long to travel and visit interesting places with loved ones. These hopes motivated him to take daily walks, follow his doctor's instructions on taking medicines, and get health checks.

There's a Chinese saying, "The cart will find its way around the hill when it gets there." It is not unlike the English saying, "You will cross the bridge when you get to it." Over the years, I have learned things will get better in the future no matter how overwhelming present circumstances appear. For things I can control, I will put every effort into it. For those I cannot, I remind myself the future will be brighter for me and I can face anything life brings to me.

Like many Chinese students growing up, my goal was to get good grades, attend a top college, and make my parents proud. When applying for graduate schools overseas, my first choice was the University of British Columbia in Canada, but they rejected my application. I was disappointed at the beginning. Just like what people say, "When God closes a door, he opens a window," UCLA accepted me. I did not realize how prestigious it was until the summer of 1995 when the assistant manager at the Chinese restaurant where I waitressed excitedly announced to the entire staff, "Wow! Lucy is going to UCLA, such a great school. She's so smart!" I blushed when the staff congratulated me. It opened a new path for me and changed my life.

In the summer prior to attending UCLA, I set up new goals: the first was to graduate with my master's degree within one year, and the second was to keep a tight rein on my spending. Studying at UCLA was not easy because of language barriers; it took me quite some time to follow the professors' instructions and understand homework assignments. Back then, internet resources were still very scarce, so we still relied heavily on books. I wished I could record classroom instructions and discussions. Too stingy to buy books, I borrowed nearly all of them from the library, except *Civil Engineering Manual*, which cost me over one hundred dollars.

I spent a significant amount of time in the library studying, even on weekends. Textbooks were unavailable to take home, and there was a three-hour borrowing limit. During those three hours, I made the most of my time by taking notes from the book so I could review them every day. To finish my degree within one year, I took four to five classes each quarter, and the classwork was heavy and hard. Even though my bachelor's degree was in environmental engineering, its focus was more on environmental monitoring and chemistry. All the engineering courses were unfamiliar and difficult for me. But one favorite course, which was also highly challenging, was a course in hydrology, where I was fascinated by water runoff and watershed impact. After spending countless hours on it, I finally got an A in this course.

"No, I need to go to the library to study," I replied to my friends when they invited me to a party on a Saturday.

"Come on, it's Saturday night, only three hours, and we will be back by 11 p.m.," they tried to convince me.

"Sorry, I have a lot to study for the finals. Next time," I persisted. Of course, they never invited me after hearing my rejections at least twice. I had no time to socialize with others because I spent all my time studying. Every day, my goals guided my focus. They helped me maintain awareness of my progress despite occasional forays to Santa Monica Beach to step on the sandy shores and watch the waves—one of my favorite activities. By June 1996, I had achieved my goal of completing my graduate degree within one year. I invited my parents to attend my commencement, who proudly told all their friends about my achievements.

In my pursuit of the American dream, I had two primary goals: advancing my career and raising a family.

After getting my master's and entering the workforce, I began recognizing the profound value of enhancing my communication and leadership skills. This realization led me to join Toastmasters in 2009, where I have improved these skills over the years through constant practice, learning, and the undertaking of leadership roles. In recent years, my dream of becoming a better coach led me to take coaching courses until I became a human potential certified coach in 2022.

When it came to my aspirations and goals of building and raising a family in the US, I faced immense challenges, having grown up in a very different environment and culture. Caring for aging and unwell parents added another layer of complexity to life. However, I remain committed to these goals and continue to learn and become a better mother and daughter in my personal life.

EVOLVING DREAMS AND GOALS
Similar to numerous immigrants, I aimed to adapt to my new surroundings and secure a fulfilling job. Two years after attaining my first professional role, a fresh goal emerged when my

boyfriend and I chose to marry in 1998. At the time, he was working on a Stanford University project. As fellow immigrants from China, both without green cards, we faced geographical constraints due to his pursuit of a PhD. The most viable location was the San Francisco Bay Area. This new dream of marrying and starting a family emboldened me to take a chance by requesting a relocation from the East Coast to the West Coast. As I mentioned in an earlier chapter, my boss approved my request after I summoned the courage to ask him. This experience taught me the power of asking and revealed the kindness with which many respond to such requests.

Throughout the years, I've come to understand not all our dreams and aspirations will come to fruition. It's important to remain adaptable, refrain from dwelling on unfulfilled past dreams, and acknowledge that destiny might lead us down unexpected paths. Additionally, our dreams and aspirations might naturally evolve as we progress through different phases of our careers and lives.

For instance, in 1998, I grew determined to pursue a professional engineering (PE) license—regarded as the highest standard of competence in the engineering profession. After dedicated study, I passed both portions of the rigorous exam: the first phase—the arduous five-and-a-half-hour engineer-in-training exam, and the second phase—the extensive ten-hour principles and practice of engineering exam. Armed with these accomplishments, I was ready to proceed with the formal application for the PE license.

However, after moving to the San Francisco Bay Area, I discovered that California required two additional exams for civil engineers to obtain the PE license—Engineering Surveying and Seismic Principles. Despite putting in countless hours of study, I fell short of the passing score on both exams, leaving me at a crossroads. At the same time, I realized my passion for the projects at work faded due to the limited design involvement and substantial compliance and policy paperwork. This new realization allowed me to reevaluate my career path. Did I want to continue pursuing the PE license in environmental engineering?

While adjusting to life in the San Francisco Bay Area in 1999–2000, I got drawn into the special atmosphere of Silicon Valley—the technology world. So many innovations and start-up news were emerging on TV and the internet. Some of my friends had switched to software engineering, database management, or information technology fields, which were popular due to high demand. After consulting with several friends and assessing my skill sets, I boldly decided to abandon my environmental engineering career and transition into quantitative analysis in the insurance industry. I based this decision on my strengths in math, computers, engineering, and market demand. This shift allowed me to explore a new passion and set new career goals.

I learned we shouldn't beat ourselves up when we can't reach our goals because we can always find or adjust to new ones. Life is ever-changing, and our interests may shift, leading us to new and exciting goals. Throughout the years, my dreams and goals have shifted from seeking a high-paying job and climbing the corporate ladder to making a positive impact on the community, especially professional women, Asian Americans, youth development, and immigrant communities.

MY FRIENDS' STORIES

Over the years, the resilience of many outstanding individuals around me has been an inspiration to me. I have seen how dreams can ignite a powerful momentum that propels immigrants forward much further than anticipated by many.

My friend, Sophia, grew up with eight siblings in the Virgin Islands during the 1970s–1990s. In a household led by her fisherman father and hardworking seamstress mother, who had also worked stints at restaurants and laundromats, the family grappled with the challenges of making ends meet. Consistent meals were a rarity; Sophia's mother often sacrificed her own sustenance to ensure her children had enough to eat. Amid the trials, she held her dream firmly: to secure a college education and pursue the path of knowledge.

After successfully gaining admission to a college in the US, Sophia pursued her dream of receiving a quality education. While studying diligently, she took on various odd jobs, such as working as a waitress, cashier, and even delivering newspapers to cover tuition and expenses. Despite her relentless efforts, life threw an unexpected curveball at Sophia. One day, she found herself unable to afford the rent for the upcoming month. Rather than burden her family or friends with her situation, she made the difficult choice to live in her car. For the next three months, she became a homeless college student. She spent her days at the school gym for showers and at the library for studying. She spent her nights sleeping in her car after finishing her work. Around the three-month mark, some of Sophia's friends discovered her predicament. Their warm-hearted response was immediate, offering her a place to stay. Their generosity and support gave her the chance to regain stability. She was deeply grateful for the kindness of her friends during this tough period. Sophia continued to stay with one of her friends temporarily until she managed to secure a place of her own that fit within her budget. From that experience, she learned to ask for help and realized people were kind and willing to help others.

When I discussed with Sophia the reason why she did not give up studying while being homeless, she said her dream of graduating from college motivated her to persist. Intent on obtaining a good education, her dream kept her spirit high and positive throughout this difficult experience.

Fast forward twenty years later, Sophia has become an accomplished Human Resources executive, a book author, and a TEDx speaker. Adding to her achievements, she recently earned a PhD in leadership and management. Balancing a demanding full-time job with the responsibilities of being a mother to two children, she continues to navigate life's challenges, driven by the very dream that has been her guiding light.

Let's look at my friend, Sheana, and her goals, hopes, and dreams.

Born in Sri Lanka, Sheana is a senior leader in B2B marketing. Very headstrong and independent at a young age, she told her parents she would move to the US one day. Finally, at the age of eighteen, her dream came true as she headed to Ohio for college.

Since she majored in political science in college, she considered working on Capitol Hill. But after enduring a painful divorce, she embraced a marketing role at a small consulting firm in the coal industry. Starting from scratch, she learned everything new, including launching their first website, creating a marketing structure, and so on. Her hard work paid off, resulting in multiple promotions. This experience ignited her passion for marketing, leading her to abandon her political aspirations.

She moved around across various sectors: power, utilities, oil, gas, etc. During the course of her career for the past twenty years, her passion and dream gave her the motivation to work hard, lead businesses, and create value for the companies. Like many other professionals, she experienced layoffs, not once, but four within eight years. Speaking of the coping mechanism and mindset, she said, "I really enjoy what I'm doing. I feel like I have so much to give to other companies and other teams that haven't found my potential. So, from a professional point of view, I just feel like I have so much to give, and I'm so excited to do the work." This kind of hope and passion pushed her forward.

Let's turn to the story of my friends, Pat and Steve, who are some of the most incredible people I know. I first met Pat at work at the environmental consulting company in 1999, when I transferred from Buffalo to San Francisco.

Pat's interest in the disability community began in high school. She said she "came across an opportunity to work at Sonoma State Hospital during my high school year. Ten students spent two weeks living there to work with patients with disabilities. We helped feed some patients, assisted with physical therapy, and read to them. Some of them had developmental issues, e.g., Down syndrome. Some of them were blind or deaf. I got to know them personally." She continued, "My interest in them grew over the years. I wrote about disabled people and institutions, as well as disability and media, when I went to college. In the 1980s, President Reagan closed down the mental institutions but didn't provide adequate care in the community. Some people with psychiatric issues had nowhere to go. That's another reason for the high rate of unhoused people. They needed psychiatric care and a safe place to live."

When Pat met her husband Steve in 1988, he was using a wheelchair because of a car accident in the 1970s that caused a spinal cord injury when he was twenty. He understood the issues of people with disabilities and decided to become a disability activist. He participated in the San Francisco 504 sit-in, which eventually led to the passing of the Rehabilitation Act that protected the rights of disabled individuals. Kind, humorous, and active, Steve always had a positive attitude and wanted to do more to help others. Pat studied disability history during graduate study, including media portrayals of disabled people. The same dream of helping the disabled community brought the two together. Pat and Steve got married in 1990. They launched a website, disabilityhistory.org, that collects and provides resources and information on disability history and culture.

I admired Pat, not only because she was friendly and offered assistance when I began my work in San Francisco, but also because she adopted two disabled girls from China. It was my fifth year in the US, and I was still adjusting to life in this new country. When she mentioned she was about to adopt a girl from China, I immediately felt closer to her. She asked me to go over some of the documents about the baby she and Steve were going to adopt. I was surprised to see the document stated the baby was blind. I thought Pat did not notice the issue because the original document in Chinese was not translated correctly. However, the picture of the baby clearly showed she was blind in one eye, and I was hesitant to point it out. But I saw the English document clearly stating the blindness of the eye. No record of her biological parents existed. The only record available showed the cause of her blindness was an earlier accident when she was a baby.

Pat seemed to understand my concerns, so she told me she was aware of it. She and Steve intentionally informed the agency they wanted a baby with a disability. Actually, they were looking for someone with a more severe disability. That shocked and puzzled me. When most people adopt a child, they usually want a healthy one. They examined the details of the documents thoroughly to make sure the future baby was healthy enough, which was understandable. Pat explained to me she and her husband were active in the disability rights community and knew many successful and happy disabled adults, so they felt prepared to parent disabled children. They also understood the difficulty for a disabled child to find an adoptive family and feel loved.

In May 1999, Pat flew to China to adopt Rosa from the Hunan Province after all the approvals and processing of paperwork. Rosa was one and a half years old and living in an orphanage. A friend of Pat's organized a welcome party for her after bringing her back to the US. I attended the party along with other friends and coworkers. People gave sincere wishes to Rosa and Pat's family. It was a touching moment to see this little girl running around like a bird and laughing. She was a girl with loving parents, just like other kids. Later on, Pat took her to see eye doctors for regular check-ups and consultations. Eventually, Rosa got a prosthetic eye. Her viable eye adapted, so she now has near-normal vision.

In 2004, Pat and Steve adopted another girl, Hannah, who was legally blind. She was twelve years old and living in the same orphanage as Rosa. Again, I was surprised, especially since I had two daughters of my own, four and two years old. I was working full-time and exhausted from taking care of them when I came home each day. I could not imagine the difficulties of raising two disabled children. If there was already a good deal of work involved with raising Rosa, whose one eye needed extra attention, I could hardly imagine the additional work required for bringing up Hannah. She arrived in a strange country at the age of twelve and was completely blind, which meant her parents needed to put in extra effort to care for her. I had no words to describe my mixed feelings for my dear friend Pat.

Working as a librarian, Steve collected a lot of books, documents, and photos, including rare pieces over the years. He was a good father to both Rosa and Hannah. After adopting Rosa, Steve worked around the house to take care of her while Pat continued working. In 2012, Steve passed away after his health deteriorated. The family and friends mourned deeply about losing such a kind soul, a dreamer but a fierce fighter for disability rights. Pat donated Steve's collections to several organizations so his legend could continue. She still maintains the website disabilityhistory.org, and her next big project is working with a group to establish a national museum of disability history and culture. I am excited about this project and admire her for her courage to continue telling and sharing stories about remarkable people with disabilities. Many of us hope her dream will come true, just like her dream of adopting two beautiful girls from China.

For Pat and Steve, their dream of giving love to two disabled children motivated them to overcome all the difficulties in life. This is part of their big dream of helping the disabled community and helping them live with respect and dignity.

How about the dreams of Hannah herself? After her adoption by Pat and Steve in 2004, Hannah graduated from UC Davis with a double major in International Relations and Chinese. She is working as the marketing operations associate at Disability:IN, while training for cycling to compete internationally. Hannah is a member of Team USA. At the August 2023 International Cycling Competition in Scotland, Hannah, along with her tandem cycling partner, won the bronze medal in the 1,000-meter sprint. The previous year, at the 2022 Para-Cycling Track World Championship in France, she won sixth in the kilo and fifth in the 200-meter sprint. From an orphan from China to a US national champion, what an amazing journey she's taken. Her biggest dream now is the Olympics in Paris in 2024 and in Los Angeles in 2028. She's such an unstoppable young woman with a big dream in her heart.

Goals are more specific than hopes and dreams, forming the central components of actions and steps, whereas hopes and dreams are less determinate. Any hopes and dreams will need to be realized through actual goals—our human efforts.

Sometimes, our hopes and dreams may come to our mind first before we sit down to create specific goals.

GUIDELINES

When we face life's challenges, we tend to forget our goals, hopes, and dreams. We feel that they are too distant to reach, making us feel frustrated, anxious, and even desperate. How can we keep our hopes and dreams undiminished during difficult times?

FIRST, I TALK POSITIVELY TO MYSELF AND TOWARD OTHERS.

It's my personal way of staying connected with my values and aspirations. Just like when I spoke at the high school event, I engaged in self-dialogue to tap into my inner thoughts. Having a conversation with ourselves might feel odd, but we've all done it at some point. When I'm alone, I find myself voicing my thoughts aloud. I realized the potency of our words through my daughter's linguistics teacher, who shared, "Your words hold immense power. Choose words that are kind, loving, positive, uplifting, encouraging, and life-affirming." This resonates deeply with me. Criticism can deflate and discourage us, while praise uplifts and motivates us. Embracing positive language helps us shift from an internal critic to an internal coach and source of comfort.

Imagine the following negative thoughts:

- I'll never get a job in my field.

- I am stupid.

- I will fail my test.

How about changing these into positive talks?

- I found good jobs in the past. What will I do to get another one?

- What I just did was less than brilliant, but I am still a smart person.

- I don't want to fail my test. I'll put in another hour to study.

I have learned to add "yet" at the end of my sentence and "will be able to" in the next sentence. In the past, I might have said, "I'm not good at writing." But now, I've shifted it to "I'm not good at writing yet. I'll keep practicing, and I will be able to improve."

This positive approach has been transformative in shifting my perspective. For instance, I used to tell myself, "No one will like my book because it's about immigrants." Now, I've shifted to saying, "Immigrants will appreciate my book, and even some nonimmigrants might find value in it, too, as it's about building resilience."

The power of positive speech goes beyond just words; it affects our stress levels and enhances our mental and physical well-being. As Andrew Bennett asserts in his TEDx Talk, "What we speak is what we create." Our brain listens to our words, so it's crucial to address ourselves kindly and optimistically. This practice fuels our ability to dream big.

Furthermore, speaking positively toward our friends and family encourages them to get in touch with their inner values and dreams as well. Moreover, it helps us build strong relationships with others.

SECOND, I ENGAGE IN REFLECTION.
Engaging in reflection is a valuable habit that allows us to glean lessons from life's challenges, particularly when we face failures, disappointments, or setbacks. It's during these tough moments that our growth often surpasses that of our successes. As part of my own practice, I often pose the following questions to myself:

- What went wrong?

- What were the reasons?

- How can I do it differently?

- Who can I ask for help?

- What can I do now to make things better?

- What would the future look like in one month or one year?

These questions serve to shift my focus from upset feelings to a more resourceful mindset. Through reflection, I cultivate the ability to forgive others and myself for errors or challenging situations. Self-reflection also allows me to get in touch with my emotions, especially during periods of vulnerability and defeat. Recognizing and understanding negative emotions becomes the initial step toward self-compassion. Consequently, self-reflection becomes a mechanism for fortifying our core values and aspirations, ensuring our dreams remain undiminished.

THIRD, I MAKE A LIST OF THINGS AND POST THESE ON MY DESK.
Dreams remain mere aspirations unless we translate them into reality through incremental, achievable actions. Personally, I have a routine of reviewing my daily planner and calendar toward my goals. This practice helps me to effectively prioritize my tasks during the day. Each morning, I make a list of tasks to accomplish for the day. These smaller tasks not only appear less daunting due to their simplicity, but they also carry a sense of familiarity. Our brain is naturally receptive to straightforward and recognizable tasks, making them easier to tackle and accomplish. According to *Psychology Today*, if something is familiar, we have clearly survived exposure to it, and our brain, recognizing this, steers us toward it. Thus, one could say we are hardwired to feel that the "known devil is better than the unknown angel." Making such a checklist can translate difficult issues into easy issues (Raghunathan 2012)

As I complete each task throughout the day, I cross out the tasks from my tasks list. Crossing out the tasks one by one is the moment for celebration. The action of checking off tasks one by one is a powerful reminder of my progress. It's a practice that has enabled me to realize numerous goals in life.

To live an abundant life, we need to have goals, hopes, and dreams. These elements infuse our existence with meaning and purpose, propelling us to explore the world around us and inspiring us to reach for an improved future. Flexibility in adapting our goals cultivates resilience, enabling us to relish life's offerings. With aspirations and dreams, we may take incremental steps to overcome life's obstacles and move forward.

CHAPTER 7

PRINCIPLE 3: GRATEFULNESS AND CONTENTMENT

———

Gratitude can transform common days into thanksgivings, turn routine jobs into joy, and change ordinary opportunities into blessings.

—WILLIAM ARTHUR WARD

One of my favorite Chinese idioms is *a blessing in disguise* (塞翁失马). Once upon a time, an old stableman and his family lived around the Great Wall in Northern China. When his horse ran off on its own, everyone felt bad for the stableman, trying to console him. But he said, "How do you know if it's not lucky?"

After a few months, his horse returned home with a new horse. Everyone felt happy for him, congratulating the old stableman. But he said again, "How do you know if this is not the start of a calamity?"

His son loved horseback riding, but one day, he fell off the horse and broke his leg. Again, everyone felt bad for the old man and comforted him again. But he said again, "How do you know this is a misfortune?"

A year flew by, and a large troop of foreign soldiers invaded the Great Wall area, so the region started enlisting young men to fight the war. The military did not recruit the stableman's son due to his broken leg. Nine out of ten people from the nearby area who fought died, while many returned home with severe injuries. Sparing the old stableman's son, he lived quite happily with his father.

The lesson is that although you may suffer a loss for a while, you may also gain unexpected benefits. The story also indicates that where there's uncertainty about life—something perceived as good might turn to misfortune, and vice versa.

In this ever-changing world, we encounter situations beyond our control—sometimes positive and sometimes negative. When faced with challenges, a content mindset and a grateful heart allow us to shift our perspective from the negative to the positive aspects of life. Therefore, one of the seven principles of building resilience is being grateful and contented.

FACTS ABOUT GRATEFULNESS AND CONTENTMENT

Both gratitude and contentment bring people many benefits in health and relationships, including increased happiness, improved mental well-being, and improved resilience.

Gratitude means appreciation for what life offers. It helps us change our focus from a perceived lack to sufficiency when we face life's challenges while comforting us with the understanding we have already gained so much from life. During difficult times, gratitude allows us to change our mindset from victim to victor and from hopelessness to hope.

Dr. Robert A. Emmons, the world's leading scientific expert on gratitude and a professor at the University of California, Davis, states, "In the face of demoralization, gratitude has the power to energize. In the face of brokenness, gratitude has the power to heal. In the face of despair, gratitude has the power to bring hope. In other words, gratitude can help us cope with hard times" (Emmons 2013).

Dr. Samuel Koranteng-Pipim believes a heart full of gratitude is a fountain from which life's richest blessings flow. Feeling blessed helps people develop a mindset of abundance, which allows them to navigate challenges and setbacks with greater resilience and optimism. Feeling content is a blessing and related to joy. He observes that the key to gratitude is contentment, and a content heart is a grateful heart (Koranteng-Pipim 2015). Experiencing contentment signifies fulfillment of life's necessities, leading to a sense of being blessed and joyful.

The article "What is Gratitude and Why Is It So Important?" under *Positive Psychology* defines gratitude as an emotion similar to appreciation and, more specifically, defines this phenomenon as a sense of happiness and thankfulness in response to a fortunate happenstance or tangible gift (Millacci 2017). Gratitude, according to the PERMA model established by Martin Seligman, the widely acknowledged father of positive psychology, is an important component of positive emotion, which in turn ranks as one of the five essential elements for well-being; the other four elements include engagement, relationships, meaning, and accomplishments.

Other researchers, such as Dr. Joshua Brown and Dr. Joel Wong, draw a similar conclusion that gratitude works to improve our mental health. Through an article published under *Mind and Body*, they shed light on a significant connection between feelings of gratitude and distinct brain activity, setting it apart from feelings of guilt. Their research validates that people who are generally more grateful show greater neural sensitivity in the medial prefrontal cortex, a brain area associated with learning and decision-making, when contributing more money to a cause (Brown and Wong 2017). Feeling grateful prompts individuals to engage in acts of paying it forward and offering assistance to others due to the positive emotions and empathy associated with gratitude.

Psychology Today suggests similar findings, stating, "Life satisfaction, empathy, compassion, feeling less lonely and more connected to others, gratitude—and more positive emotions—may all be linked in the prefrontal cortex" (Khorrami 2020).

Harvard Medical School reports that gratitude is strongly and consistently associated with greater happiness because gratitude helps people feel more positive emotions, relish good experiences, improve their health, deal with adversity, and build strong relationships (Harvard Medical School 2021). Similarly, David DiPaola, a national board-certified health and wellness coach, believes gratitude and contentment can lead to happiness, health, and success when practiced regularly over time, and gratefulness inspires positive thinking and hope (DiPaola 2023). Jacqueline D. Pearce, a licensed mental health counselor, also defines contentment as being happy with what you have, who you are, and where you are. It respects the reality of the present and trusts that future outcomes will be positive (Pearce 2023). Five benefits emphasize the significance of contentment:

- Peace of mind: Contentment fosters a positive mindset that supports personal growth and improvement. It doesn't mean giving up on dreams but finding peace with the present, which, in turn, enhances motivation for a better future.

- Happiness: Contentment leads to happiness by letting go of cravings for what is lacking. Acceptance of the current situation breeds happiness, as gratitude for existing blessings outweighs preoccupation with unmet desires.

- Stronger relationships: Contentment extends to accepting others as they are, which can strengthen relationships. It encourages trust, appreciation, and growth, nurturing more fulfilling connections.

- Distinguishing wants and needs: Contentment helps differentiate between desires and necessities. Recognizing that material possessions aren't the ultimate source of joy enables a focus on inner contentment rather than external accumulation.

- Simplicity: Contentment promotes a simpler life by curbing the constant need for more. This reduces stress, allowing individuals to prioritize personal growth and inner peace over material possessions.

In summary, amid tough times, gratitude directs our focus to the positive and functional aspects rather than dwelling on shortcomings. This shift trains our minds to seek positivity, making challenges feel more manageable. Contentment, the feeling of satisfaction, helps us embrace difficulties as part of life. Gratitude and contentment are mutually reinforcing; gratitude enhances contentment, and vice versa.

MY FRIENDS' EXPERIENCES

Most of my accomplished friends have shared with me their profound gratitude for their families and friends, particularly during adversity. Their expressions of thankfulness served as a source of solace and acted as a buffer against the stresses of life's difficulties. Gratitude has become one of the sources of strength and power.

My friend Yasmin is a perfect example of a person with a thankful heart. Working as a senior consultant in the financial industry, she recalled the difficulties she encountered when taking care of her cancer-stricken mother, an immigrant from Japan. She was grateful to her for being the most influential person in her life. Her mother not only had a strong faith but was also stoic. When Yasmin was little, her mother chose to stay with the kids even though her marriage was failing. After years of hard work, her mother was happy to see her children grow up and was finally going to relax and enjoy her life—until she was diagnosed with lung cancer in 2003. Since Yasmin wanted to take care of her mother, she decided to have her mother move in with her. She then talked with her boss about possibly moving her office from San Francisco to Walnut Creek, which was much closer to where she lived—two blocks from the hospital. As Yasmin got the approval, viewing it as a *miracle of God*, she felt grateful for her boss's kindness.

In the third year, Yasmin faced another challenging battle as her mother developed independent breast cancer. In addition to battling with insurance companies, she took on the main caregiver role, bringing her to the ER and draining the fluid from her lungs. Recalling those stressful days, Yasmin admits, "I used to be a very sound sleeper, and I had to listen for sounds (from my mom)... so that was very tough."

However, she felt fortunate she had her siblings and good friends by her side. At least there was someone there to talk to and give emotional support, easing some of the burdens she carried. She was also grateful to her mother for trying to help out too. Yasmin recalled that, "Whatever my mom could do, like cleaning the house, preparing food—she did it all. Even at the very end, when she couldn't cook anymore, she would write the shopping list for the week. I remember going to the grocery store the first time we didn't have a shopping list..." Throughout this journey, Yasmin learned the true value of a support network, cherishing the people who were there for her during those difficult times.

Similarly, my dear friend Xing always holds deep gratitude for her parents' unwavering support and encouragement.

Much like numerous other Chinese students pursuing higher education overseas in the 1990s, Xing came to the US for her master's degree in a STEM field. Within two years, she earned her degree from a prestigious university and secured a position in Silicon Valley in 2000. Curious about her success, I asked about the factors contributing to her achievements. Reflecting on her journey, she responded, "It's all thanks to my parents. They instilled in me the importance of education from a young age. It was my dad who urged me to continue my studies after college. I embarked on this journey to the US because of their support. They opened the door to the world beyond, uplifting me from the confines of a small town in China." Later on, her parents played a pivotal role in caring for her two children as she navigated her career in the competitive realm of Silicon Valley.

For Xing, the most profound influence from her parents was the values they ingrained in her—courage and integrity. "Three years ago, I spoke up at the Cupertino Public Hearing against a proposal for planning marijuana stores near schools. It was a moment of courage I never thought I had. I'm really proud of myself," she recounted. Her eyes gleamed behind her glasses as she continued, "I shared a family tale from the early 1900s about my great-grandfather's struggles with opium addiction, which tore apart both his health and his family. 'Never get near it!' My father passed this story on to me, and I'm determined to keep my kids and other children away from its harm." Ultimately, her efforts played a part in the rejection of the proposed marijuana store near schools. Despite this being her first public speaking experience, she stood up for what felt right, displaying remarkable boldness.

This deeply rooted courage resulted from the values her parents instilled in her, and for this, she has an enduring gratitude toward them. To Xing, her actions not only safeguarded her own children but also extended to the well-being of other children. These values are set to endure and be handed down from generation to generation. Her deep appreciation for her parents has been a driving force, propelling her to overcome numerous challenges in life, and her resilience brilliantly reflects this gratitude.

MY PARENTS' EXPERIENCES

A man who is content will be happy. My parents, exemplars of contentment, instilled in me the essence of finding joy in life's gifts. I have learned from them that happiness blooms from within, nurtured by a grateful heart.

Growing up as an orphan, Mom did not know her birthdate because no one around her mentioned it. Her only certainty was her birth year—a time when her father embarked on a war-bound journey. In the aftermath of the wars, many like her lacked formal birth documents, leaving their birthdays unmarked. By the time she went to Beijing and applied for middle school, she realized she needed an official birthdate.

"Even your grandparents never mentioned your birthday? No one celebrated it for you?" I asked Mom.

"No one... So, I picked June 1 as my birthday and wrote it on the document." With no trace of regret in her voice, she added with a smile, "Because it's International Children's Day—a day to be happy."

One would think how sad it was that no one knew or celebrated her birthday and that she had to pick up her own birthday. But it was quite the opposite. She was pleased she got to choose her own birthday—and have it coincide with a happy yet meaningful day.

Even though she envied those friends who lived with their parents, she enjoyed her time spent at her relatives' houses. She loved her grandparents, who helped raise her after the early loss of her mother. She remembered she used to help her grandmother pick red and plum dates from the tall tree, one of the rare memories she can recall today. When her grandparents passed away a few years later, she appreciated her uncles and aunts, who allowed her to stay with them for a few months at a time despite the reality of pervasive poverty and anxiety when few could feed their own children. When she told me these stories, she sounded like she barely suffered. If anything, she had happy recollections of playing with her cousins around the house. To this day, Mom remains grateful for the care of her relatives during those tumultuous times, particularly her father's youngest sister—her aunt, who not only transformed her life but also stood by her side during significant milestones in her life.

Similarly, Dad always felt fortunate to have a loving family despite their poverty. He was very close to his grandmother, who not only saved his life during the war but also saved the best morsels of food for him. He recalled how she always wished him well at school each morning and welcomed him home when he returned. She repeated the same routine for years till he became a full-grown man and started working. Dad felt even more grateful for her continuing care after his wedding. Seeing that my mom was pregnant, she got excited and started making baby clothes for my brother, finishing one set a month before his birth. Content with the completion of her task, she passed away peacefully in a few days. Each time Dad retold this story to me, he was full of emotion, always expressing his gratitude for such a loving grandmother. "She was the kindest person. I was her eldest grandson; she cherished me deeply."

My memories of my paternal grandmother remain faint, as I was merely six years old when she departed from this world. My parents, however, held her in high regard for the support she extended during my brother's infancy despite her own ailing health. Though her illness limited her capabilities, her aid was invaluable in those early months, allowing my parents to maintain their work commitments. When my grandmother suffered a fall that resulted in a broken hip, my parents invited her to our home to take care of her during her final months. Surrounded by her loved ones, she passed away peacefully the following year.

It's important for us to remember blessings in our lives. My parents believed they had many good times, bad times, and in between. In fact, one could say their contentment was their greatest blessing. They always focused on the little things and moments that made them happy while celebrating minor victories that some might deem frivolous. I have learned from them that even if most of our days are as plain as water while exciting moments are rare, a truly happy person is one who manages to find joy in every ordinary day. My parents used to take my brother and me to a nearby park to play. Under the bright sun, we ran around the trees and flowers with laughter and chased each other. How beautiful the blue skies and shining sun were in those days! Some days, Mom would stay at home to wash, clean, and cook while Dad took us to catch tiny fish from the river. Returning home with a hungry stomach, we devoured the meals that Mom prepared for us. My parents would watch us inhale our food, feeling so satisfied with those moments. We can choose to be happy as happiness comes from the heart and our awareness of gratitude.

Gratitude not only brings happiness but also peace and empathy. Just as Mom felt she had so many blessings, she also felt sorry for those who were less fortunate. Sometimes, others wronged her or took advantage of her because of her gentle manners and kindness. But she would only be unhappy for a short period of time before forgiving others. At one time, her colleague borrowed money from her—about one hundred Yuan she had received for her research achievements, and never returned it to her. He later explained he was very short on money. Perhaps because Mom understood the man had two children to raise, she did not harbor any grudges even though she patiently waited for him to return the money.

Back then, even ten Yuan was a lot of money because Mom was only making fifty-six Yuan per month—the standard salary for those working at her research institute. That's only equivalent to a few US dollars. The living cost back in the 1980s was quite low in China. Even though one hundred Yuan was nearly twice her monthly salary, she believed she already had a lot of blessings—her health, a loving husband and children, and her career. Instead, she pitied the man, believing he must be struggling to support his family. So, she never accused him of any wrongdoing and never pressed him for her money again. Her sense of gratitude helped her maintain inner peace while rendering her empathetic to others.

Dad never forgot those people who helped him either. He believed "A drop of water in need shall be returned with a spring indeed." It's a famous Chinese idiom urging people to help others. He deeply appreciated their help during his difficult times—and often reminded us we needed to try our best to help them back.

For those instances where my parents couldn't reciprocate or directly show their gratitude, they carried those memories with them, and they shared them with me over the years. Dad often recounted the time his uncle gave him a bowl of noodles when he was on the brink of starvation as a child. He talked about the kind priest who provided him with toothpowder that saved his infected leg and his schoolteacher who pushed him to explore Chinese literacy. Mom spoke about how crucial her aunt's care proved in overcoming a serious illness, how generously her old neighbors looked after my infant brother, and how inspiring her music teacher was in recognizing her singing talent and encouraging her to pursue her passion. A radiant smile graced Mom's face when she shared these heartwarming tales.

Even though those events occurred many years ago, they told them again and again as if they happened just yesterday. The stories enhanced my parents' belief that they were very fortunate in life and surrounded by kind people. Counting these past blessings helped them trust the goodness in people in life.

Like Charles Dickens said, "Reflect upon your present blessings, of which every man has plenty; not on your past misfortunes, oh which all men have some" (Dickens 1836). The more people count their blessings, the more they feel grateful; the more they feel grateful, the more they find their blessings. Feeling grateful and counting blessings is a good cycle for happiness.

With grateful hearts, my parents extended their love to those they did not know. One of the charities they admired was the Hope Project in China, the largest nonprofit organization that helps children from low-income families get an education. They had a strong desire to give back and support underprivileged children with limited access to education. This was their way of expressing gratitude for their own educational opportunities.

Besides giving donations, they volunteered at their church as librarians for over six years until they had to give up in their late seventies because they became too old to bend down to sort the books. During those years, they treated their volunteering work as a real job, diligently maintaining the bookshelves in neat order while managing the borrowing and returning process joyfully. They enjoyed taking care of the books as if they were their pets and often expressed their gratitude with smiles and happy interactions with others.

With life's uncertainty, Dad told me to have an easy mind. There's always something we cannot control in life. No matter what happens in life, he said, you should remain calm and accept it with optimism. There's always a bright side. There's always a lesson you can learn. Dad's contentment helped him to accept reality, let go of worries, and adapt to a difficult life.

During the Cultural Revolution, Dad, along with other intellectuals, was sent to cadre school for reeducation. Cadre schools were intended by Chairman Mao to reeducate cadres and intellectuals to perform manual labor, grow their own food, and undergo ideological reeducation. Cadres would take turns going to the villages or grass-roots levels to gain first-hand experience in productive work. Living conditions in these schools were usually quite challenging for students, especially since many were used to a less strenuous life (*Chineseposters.net* 2023).

Dad and his colleagues had to learn from local peasants by working hard in the fields every day. Because of the strenuous work, they felt exhausted at the end of the day. Dad accepted the fact and tried his best to enjoy the time there. He was glad he had the opportunity to learn new skills, e.g., raising pigs. He liked his pigs very much while, in turn, his pigs recognized him. Every day, he put out the food for them and cleaned out their manure. He felt fulfilled as a farmer and enjoyed seeing his pigs grow larger. He was also glad his work helped him build his muscles and grow stronger, especially since he was already tall. He was proud of being able to carry heavy loads using a shoulder pole since they were as heavy as those of local farmers.

He was also content with the food. Because of hard labor, he ate a lot—often eight steamed buns and two bowls of rice soup during each meal. Although there was not much food other than steamed buns and rice soup, he was satisfied with the quantity. During his free moments, he dedicated himself to learning English. On less hectic days, he would allocate thirty minutes to an hour in the early morning, reciting English words and sentences before anyone else was awake. It was intrinsic to his character to invest his time in acquiring new knowledge. While maintaining a contented mindset, Dad embraced whatever life presented, but this didn't equate to relinquishing his aspirations and passions.

DAD'S LAST DAYS FILLED WITH GRATITUDE

Expressing gratitude and contentment is simple in words, yet far more challenging to truly feel, especially amid life-and-death circumstances. At the beginning of 2021, after almost one year of the hiatus due to COVID-19, I felt a sense of relief as my parents became part of the first wave to receive their COVID-19 vaccination shots, coupled with the anticipation of the pandemic's eventual end. However, Dad fell ill and went to the ICU one day before Thanksgiving 2021. Anxiety once again gripped me as I grappled with concern for his well-being and the treatment he needed.

Eventually, Dad transferred to a nursing center, which operated following the stringent COVID-19 rules. Compounding our challenges, the center's abrupt closure due to a COVID-19 case left us utterly helpless and disconnected from him. In the face of his health struggles, Dad's fragility made the prospect of disconnection from us seem an almost cruel fate for him to endure. The medical team proposed hospice care, acknowledging the final stage of his life, a reality that shook me to my core. Feeling exhausted and desperate, I experienced sleepless nights. A tumultuous blend of guilt, anger, and hopelessness washed over me.

Thankfully, my close friends reminded me of the power of gratitude. Amid the challenges, I realized frustration wouldn't help. Instead, I focused on being grateful for the support around me—from the medical team's care during the pandemic to the caregivers and my family's unwavering presence. With renewed determination, I wiped my tears and embraced whatever came my way.

After a complicated procedure, they granted Dad his wish to return home—a choice that reflected his strong will. He wanted his loved ones to surround him in his warm and joyful home. Even though Dad spent most of his time sleeping, he was awake and looked peaceful on the rolling bed when he was sent home via ambulance. On December 21, 2021, just four days before Christmas, he was finally home after one month away. He thanked the emergency paramedics team and bid them farewell with a wave. At that moment, Dad's demeanor and gesture served as a poignant reminder that life is a journey we should embrace with gratitude and contentment for its offerings. His actions provided a powerful example of living as a grateful soul.

In his last days, he continued to show gratitude toward the people surrounding him. In the nursing center, he politely thanked the nurses and doctors who took care of him. After his release home, he appreciated the visiting nurses, caregivers, and our family members. At one time, my husband and the caregiver tried to use a bedsheet to lift him up to transfer him from one bed to another. They were trying to put an air mattress on the bed. Dad awoke because of the move and looked worried. My husband and the caregiver comforted him by ensuring him this move was safe and not to worry about falling. Dad still gestured to everyone with a facial expression of concern. Finally, he raised both his hands and pointed to his waist and then pointed to my husband's waist. My husband suddenly understood Dad's concern; Dad worried about my husband spraining his waist when carrying Dad's heavyweight. My husband told Dad not to worry much because he was not heavy at all. It was true he had lost a lot of weight in the past three weeks. Observing them, I could not hold my tears from streaming down. Even though Dad was too weak to talk and breathe on his own, he was concerned about others. He truly appreciated everyone around him and showed his gratitude and grace till the end of his life.

On Christmas Day, my three children arrived to sing Christmas carols for Grandma and Grandpa. I woke up Dad so he could enjoy the heartwarming performance. He smiled at them and thanked them with a whisper. Summoning his fading strength, he managed to call each of their names. Standing by his side, tears welled in my eyes, but I brushed them away, not wanting to reveal my emotions in that delicate moment. As he gazed upon his grandchildren, he radiated a sense of tranquility, satisfaction, and peace. How I wished he could sing with us as he had in previous years! In the following days, he remained serene and content until he peacefully passed away on January 3, 2022. Dad led a life suffused with gratitude and contentment, serving as a testament to the art of resilient living.

GUIDELINES
Cultivating gratitude is a beautiful practice that enriches our lives in various ways. Here are a few ways to embrace and express gratitude:

FIRST, KEEP A JOURNAL

Maintaining a journal offers a meaningful way to connect with our emotions and experiences. The reflection prompts within the journal provide a space to delve deep into our thoughts and feelings. Through writing, we can gain clarity and insight into our inner world. While I don't write in my journal every day, I turn to it during challenging moments, finding solace in expressing myself. My journal has become a trusted companion, always ready to listen with compassion. Like a supportive friend, it's a channel for both sharing my struggles and celebrating my achievements, reminding me of the blessings I've been fortunate to count.

SECOND, EXPRESS GRATITUDE THROUGH MESSAGES AND LETTERS

The practice of sending letters of appreciation holds immense value, a lesson I learned from my parents and later my daughters' school. Witnessing my daughters write and draw messages to parent volunteers after their field trips highlighted the power of expressing gratitude. This practice enriches our relationships and serves as a potent reminder of the blessings in our lives. As Dr. Laurie Santos at Yale University suggests, we need to make time for gratitude, such as writing a gratitude letter to others, and it will increase our happiness. She found that writing a letter of gratitude and delivering it in person is an effective practice because the act makes the recipient cherish the moment and can also boost the sender's happiness for months (Talesnik 2020).

THIRD, GIVE BACK TO THE COMMUNITY

Discovering the joy of giving back to the community is a journey of self-discovery. Volunteering stands as a transformative way to actively contribute to our surroundings.

Beyond expressing our gratitude, it fosters a deep sense of connection with others. Moreover, volunteering helps us boost our self-esteem and overall satisfaction as we recognize the positive impact of our contributions.

Gratitude fosters happiness, honors moments, and acknowledges others. Contentment embraces fate with tranquility, epitomized by the Chinese adage, "Don't be surprised by favor or disgrace; watch the flowers bloom and fall in front of the court." When flowers bloom, we appreciate the vitality and beauty of the flowers; when flowers wither, we observe the natural cycle of the flowers' life. Understanding that life has ups and downs helps us to take it easy and remain calm when misfortune arrives. Understanding life's uncertainty helps us have an easy mind. With an easy mind, we accept what life throws at us and cherish the joyful moments in life. Through gratitude and contentment, we sculpt a mindset that navigates challenges and treasures joys with grace.

CHAPTER 8

PRINCIPLE 4: SPIRITUALITY AND FAITH

———

Faith is the strength by which a shattered
world shall emerge into the light.
—HELEN KELLER

Religion and spirituality have been two primary components of Chinese culture and identity for centuries. Considered the *three* pillars of ancient Chinese society—Confucianism, Taoism, and Buddhism—influence the government, science, the arts, and social structure (*National Geographic* 2023). The Chinese believe, "There are gods three feet above everyone." It indicates that gods are watching everyone everywhere, and no one can get away with evil.

However, from the 1950s, Chinese students learned from the earliest grades they should embrace atheism and you should abandon beliefs in any gods as they are useless, unscientific, and old-fashioned. As such, society considered those who burned incense and prayed superstitious. Also, as the country put faith in Marxism since the founding of the New China in 1949, many adopted his belief that religion is the opium of the people as propounded by Marx in the Introduction of "A Contribution to the Critique of Hegel's Philosophy of Right" (Marx 1844). So, as schoolchildren, we learned to sing the communist song "The International," which claims there is no God in the world.

I used to believe these ideas until I became a Christian in 2004. After attending church for several years, the love of God moved my heart. Religion gave me a deeper meaning and purpose in life—more significant than this world and short life offers. My faith in God provides comfort, solace, and hope during difficult times, allowing me to feel I am not alone and know I am loved and blessed by my creator. My life has become more fulfilling, joyful, and peaceful. To me and many others, spirituality and faith are powerful principles in building resilience.

FACTS ABOUT SPIRITUALITY AND CONTENTMENT

Research proves that practicing spirituality and faith improves an overall sense of well-being and helps many overcome difficulties and build resilience. In the article "How Spirituality Can Benefit Your Health and Well-Being," Dr. Elizabeth Scott summarizes how spirituality can benefit people in four areas. First, it can help people find purpose and meaning in life. Second, it helps people cope with the effects of everyday stress. Third, people restore hope and optimism through spirituality.

Fourth, it helps people find a sense of community and support. Scott states, "Dedication to God or a higher power translated into less stress reactivity, greater feelings of well-being, and ultimately even a decreased fear of death" (Scott 2023).

Other research also shows that regular spiritual activities can improve young people's well-being. According to the Harvard School of Public Health, researchers found that those who attend weekly religious services or practiced daily prayer or meditation in their youth report greater life satisfaction and positivity in their twenties—and are less likely to subsequently have symptoms of depression, smoke, use illicit drugs, or have a sexually transmitted infection than people raised with less regular spiritual habits (Sweeney 2018). *Diverse Issues in Higher Education* also encourages students to deploy the power of faith to unlock their promise and potential. It mentions you can consider and teach faith from a religious perspective and a practical one. In short, "We can tap into it at any given time. It can be intentionally utilized for both individual and collective progress" (Bright 2021).

Also, research shows that spirituality provides a source of strength when individuals confront daunting challenges. According to the *National Library of Medicine*, religion and spirituality provide people with hope, comfort, and resilience in the face of adversity; spiritual resilience helps people have divine support, maintain purpose, and express gratitude (Manning 2014).

Other research also concludes that spirituality helps people build resilience in difficult times. Andrea Mathews, a Licensed Professional Counselor, in the article "How Spirituality

Affects Resilience," points out, "Resilience demonstrates how well we adapt to difficult life challenges, such as illness, trauma, relationship problems, workplace issues or financial stressors. Those who have a deep spirituality or are in the process of developing one can show such resilience." When referring to people undergoing challenging times, she states, "Even when life doesn't make sense, their spirituality offers them a powerful resource to lean on until they can become grounded again in reality" (Mathews 2021). These difficult times include grieving the loss of a loved one. In the "Spiritual beliefs may affect the outcome of bereavement: prospective study," published under the *National Library of Medicine*, researcher Kiri Walsh concludes, "People who profess stronger spiritual beliefs seem to resolve their grief more rapidly and completely after the death of a close person than do people with no spiritual beliefs" (Walsh et al. 2002).

Furthermore, spirituality encourages people to have better relationships with themselves, others, and the unknown. It can help people deal with stress by giving them a sense of peace, purpose, and forgiveness, thereby creating a positive impact on mental health. Spirituality and faith are the principles of building resilience because they provide numerous benefits in fostering resilience and inner strength (*WebMD* 2021).

- Offer individuals a sense of purpose and meaning

- Promote emotional well-being

- Empower people to overcome obstacles during trials and challenges

- Enhance relationships with others

It is important for us to pay attention to spiritual care in our daily lives, and extremely important when we face life's difficulties. During a major crisis such as the COVID-19 pandemic, we need to make sure that everyone is getting spiritual care (Hall 2020).

The following two touching stories from my interviews give strong evidence that spirituality or faith empowers people to go through life's darkest moments.

ANDREW BENNETT'S STORY

Andrew Bennett is a TEDx Talk speaker and a magician. His talk "The Magic of Words—What We Speak Is What We Create" amazed me with the power of belief (Bennett 2014). Although I was always aware we should encourage others using positive words, I never actually believed our words and beliefs could transform our wishes into reality.

His talk fascinated me and made me curious about how he decided to use the magic word *abracadabra* to change people's lives. Fortunately, I got the opportunity to interview Andrew, and to my surprise, his personal story touched me even deeper.

Andrew's adversity began when he was three years old after his mother and sister died at the hands of a drunk driver. One year later, his father remarried and only took his older brother, leaving him to his grandparents on his mother's side. As his grandparents started raising him, his grandfather became his best friend and taught him magic. But when Andrew was sixteen, his grandfather died by suicide, which shattered his world. A few years later, at the age of twenty-four, he lost his grandmother to spinal myelitis, after which she suffered as a quadriplegic for nine months. It threw him into a pit of despair once again. When his great-uncle—his grandmother's brother, a Baptist minister hugged him and tried to comfort him, Andrew said to his great-uncle, "Do not talk to me about your God. There's no God." Losing all those he loved—his mother, sister, father, brother, and grandparents by the age of twenty-four—he lost trust in God, believing God had abandoned him.

Fast forward fifteen years later, Andrew achieved huge success in his business through hard work and dedication. However, just when he was about to celebrate his accomplishments, tragedy struck again. His dream home became infested with toxic mold, forcing him to sue the builder, who refused to fix the problem. Andrew ran out of money to pursue the case and experienced bankruptcy, forcing him and his wife to move to a small apartment. As if fate had a cruel sense of humor, a catastrophic event occurred. One afternoon, lightning struck the roof over their bedroom and started a fire in the attic, which caused the roof to collapse, destroying everything they owned. They also lost three of their cherished cats, who were like their children. The old adage, it never rains but it pours, certainly applied to Andrew after he and his wife got divorced. Andrew described those days as the time when he really hit rock bottom. He said, "Even though I was never suicidal, I planned to move to a very remote part of Michigan and spend the rest of my life in solitude."

It was 2010, and Andrew turned fifty. He had been through extremely challenging times involving great loss in his life.

Anguish, pain, and desperation overwhelmed him. One fateful night, as he lay in bed in excruciating pain, he poured his heart out, asking, "God, why did you leave me?" To his astonishment, he heard a voice saying, "Andrew, I never left you. You left me. I'm always here. And I always love you."

The next morning, he woke up with a newfound sense of purpose and hope. He said, "For whatever reason, I was thinking about magic—*appear, disappear,* and *restore*—the first lessons you learn in magic." This profound insight became the foundation for his speaking engagements, workshops, and coaching sessions. He encouraged others to explore the power of these questions: "What do you want to make appear in your life? What needs to disappear in your life? What do you need to restore in your life?"

That night, he struggled in desperation, and God answered his cry. He received the affirmative answer that God had always loved him and never forsaken him. This love restored his strength and courage, leading him to transform himself and rebuild his life.

At the same time, he was also curious about abracadabra. He started searching online for the meaning and the etymology of the word. He couldn't find anything, so he contacted the linguistics department at MIT. MIT responded, saying they would do some research. After two or three days, Andrew was surprised to receive a phone call from Noam Chomsky, the distinguished linguist, philosopher, and political activist. Chomsky explained to Andrew that abracadabra is a word from the ancient sacred Aramaic language. Abracadabra means I create that which I speak. Andrew felt it was a little convoluted, so he shifted the wording to make it clear. He thought "What we speak is what we create" sounded clearer to people. He applied with the US Patent and Trademark Office to get a trademark on abracadabra. In the meantime, more good things began to happen. Andrew continued, "Within a year and a half, I met my wife, Jennifer, who's the greatest thing that's ever happened to me." They have been happily married for ten years now.

Andrew attributed his success in life to his experience with God. As the voice told him that night when he suffered immense pain, he discovered that God never left him. To me, the *abracadabra* was a divine sign and a gentle reminder of God's unwavering love surrounding Andrew all along. The word woke him up at the right time about his own ability of restoration and blessed him with the help he needed.

He believes faith is a magical force that saved him. He says, "I really think it's important to move beyond religion and contemplate the idea of God as a force for good that exists in every atom in the universe. That is a creative force that's constantly expanding. Sometimes, creation involves destruction. Things we see as falling apart and an ending or dying will give way to something new. So ultimately, what wins out is the creative force." He believed goodness exists everywhere, and each person is born with that goodness. He continued, "To me, God is in all of us. For the last ten years, my drive has been to just spend my life as a thank you to God. I want to spend my life honoring God. That means being the best person I can be to honor the privilege he's given me of being alive, but also about helping others. My focus is all about serving God."

The power of spirituality and faith has been Andrew's guiding light. It helped Andrew walk through his darkest moments in life and drive him to see goodness in others and devote himself to serving others. His life's journey is a testimony of the transformative magic of spirituality, creating a ripple effect of positivity and light in the world. That's truly magic.

DAISY'S STORY

Let us look at my friend Daisy's story. Daisy immigrated along with her family to America from Africa at a young age. Since she couldn't speak English, her teachers held her back in school until she learned it. As a non-white person, she found it challenging to assimilate with either Blacks or whites.

Daisy's major challenging time came with her mother's diagnosis of breast cancer. It was devastating for the family to hear from the doctor saying her mother had less than six months to live after she went through surgery.

She said, "Within those six months, my older sister and I began to care for my mother so my father could continue to work and provide for all of us. He carried the weight of the world on his shoulders. We watched as cancer took its toll on my mother and ultimately arranged home hospice care. During that time, I stopped talking to God. I was angry that he took my mom from me at a young age. I was angry he didn't heal her. She was a devout Catholic; she prayed every day and night. She was a hard worker, a delightful giver, and pure in spirit. People loved her. She was a Proverbs 31 woman. He should have protected her as I thought." A "Proverbs 31 woman" refers to a portrayal in the Bible (Proverbs 31:10–31) of an ideal wife and mother known for her strength, wisdom, industriousness, and care for her family.

She kept asking why God allowed the tragedy to happen to her mom, a loving and caring person, a compassionate Catholic, and a strenuous soul. It brought so much pain to her entire family and friends. In the midst of this, she fervently prayed and poured out her heartache to the divine, seeking solace and understanding.

The second most difficult time for her was the period when she went through a bitter divorce. She was dragged through court simply because she was the breadwinner of the family. Her ex-husband demanded more than his fair share—money he never contributed during their marriage. There were times when she was in the pit of despair when her ex-husband refused to pay for anything, which eventually left her living paycheck to paycheck until her bank account ran dry. She said, "I immersed myself in the scripture because that became my food. That's really how I became the Christian I am today." That was when God sent someone to help her. Noticing her stress and struggle, her friend sorrowfully looked at her and asked what was going on. Upon learning how destitute Daisy was in the midst of this personal battle, her friend wrote a check with $1,000, stating this money was not to be paid back. It was just the bridge Daisy needed until she landed a second job, enabling her to manage the mounting bills.

After one year and a half, Daisy thought she could not stand it anymore, and she was mentally, emotionally, and physically exhausted. Her ex-husband kept writing nasty emails and text messages to her and even waited outside her home for her as she returned home from work.

Unable to fight anymore, one night, she made a plan to take her own life. She felt guilty about what she would do. She said, "As I was apologizing for all I was about to do, for the first time in my life, I heard God's voice call to me. I was on the floor, sobbing. He said to me, 'My daughter, take one step in front of the other, and I will carry you the rest of the way.' I said, 'But I'm so tired.' He said, 'Just one step.'" While hearing her loud cry, the kids burst through the door, asking what was wrong. Pretending nothing was wrong, Daisy casually went to wash her face. She recognized the preservation of her life was by a force beyond her comprehension.

Among the stories of heartbreak, one stood out: one of the doctors she had worked with took his life because he was going through a difficult divorce. Daisy found herself pondering her own existence amid this tragic revelation. "That could have been me, but I know the Lord heard my cries," she admitted, acknowledging her own battle. She felt comfort and strength from God. And while her situation didn't improve overnight but continued for three long years, every time she floundered in despair, she would remember the Lord's deep peaceful baritone voice nudging her to take one step at a time and assuring her he would take care of the rest.

While appreciating her friend's help, she wanted to give thanks to God. Drawing inspiration from the Old Testament Bible verses that describe the devastating locust invasion on Israel's crops and how God made up for those lost years and provided harvest, she found hope in God's promise of restoration. Just as God granted abundance after destruction, she, too, experienced His blessings. She said, "God multiplied with a locust tried to destroy. In fact, that same $1,000, I've passed it on five times to many others and have walked others through their divorces, showing them how to lean on and trust in God. In the depths of my despair, God has touched me. He is a restorer, and I must continue to do for others as he did for me." She said, "God is amazing. It's so wonderful. I'm telling you that his kindness, his faithfulness, and his compassion, once you taste it, you want others to taste it… the very essence of his goodness."

That pivotal night when God's voice reached her, she found the source of kindness and power and became strong enough to reclaim her life. Through this profound encounter, Daisy found that provision does not come from man but from God Almighty and that nothing in life is wasted. She hopes her story will prompt others to lean on Christ during their darkest times, knowing He hears every prayer and wipes every tear.

Daisy walked out of the darkest moments through her faith. She has become a successful executive who continues to live a life of servitude and filled with gratitude. Compassion is not a characteristic or attribute but a lifestyle.

PERSONAL EXPERIENCES

Like many Chinese who grew up in the 1940s–1950s, my parents had little exposure to religion throughout most of their adulthood, but they believed in supernatural powers from early childhood. Mom believed her parents' spirits surrounded her and blessed her throughout her life. Dad appreciated the priest who gave him the seemingly magic medicine that saved his leg and his life.

Baptized in 2004, my husband and I became Christians after attending church for a few years and following my parents-in-law's footsteps. Two years later, my brother's family became Christians. In 2009, my parents converted to Christianity after feeling touched by God's love and salvation. They believed His grace allowed them to overcome life's challenges throughout the years. Religion supported Dad through the last thirteen years of his life and gave him the strength to fight various diseases.

My parents served as librarians for the books belonging to their church for over six years. As his health deteriorated dramatically in 2018, Dad had to give up his position. But he continued to participate in the fellowship and Sunday services. Bible verses became the nutrient source of his soul. Among his favorite verses was Psalm 23 ("The Lord is my shepherd, I shall not be in want…").

Psalm 23 is also one of my favorite Bible verses because it provides reassurance and reminders of God's loving guidance and provision in times of difficulty. Because God is like a shepherd, and He cares and leads His flock and offers comfort and protection in the face of life's challenges, I am no longer lonely. At the darkest moments in my life, I have found that God sent the right people to support and comfort me.

I used to recite Psalm 23 with Dad while he did his walking exercises with his walker in his living room. With every wobbly step he took, I couldn't help but draw a parallel to the notes of "You Raise Me Up"—the same melody that evoked memories of how he once uplifted me in my childhood. The lyrics suggest that during times of weakness, struggles, and challenges, individuals can turn to God for upliftment and guidance. The very notion of being *raised up* became a symbol of God's remarkable ability to extend comfort, fortitude, and a renewed sense of purpose in the face of life's storms. Dad, in his own remarkable way, leaned on the Lord Jesus so he could stand on the top of the mountain and walk on the stormy waves. It was through this reliance he discovered the boundless strength that comes from surpassing one's limitations.

As I look back on my journey, my heart fills with overwhelming gratitude toward God. From the very beginning, He blessed me with the most wonderful parents; their guidance and love have been my pillars of strength. Then there's Beth, my first American friend. She was like a guardian angel, always by my side, steering me forward with her unwavering belief in my abilities. In 1997, when I experienced the loneliest moments in Buffalo, especially when the contractor mocked me at work, I experienced a sudden sense of reassurance when several friends arrived to spend time with me. They were angels sent by God to wipe my tears away. Reflecting on these chapters of my life, it humbles me that God's grace has been a constant, manifesting through the love of family, the support of friends, and the unexpected arrival of angels during my moments of need.

During my children's adolescent years, I felt frustrated by their rebellions. My church sisters were always there to pray for me and give me emotional support. One night, in tears, I questioned God about the hardships. His response was simple: "Be grateful." Initially confusing, those words eventually became a guiding light, helping me find blessings within challenges. Gratitude shifted my perspective, showing me growth and love amid the struggles. It was a transformative lesson in finding light even in the toughest times.

Another painful chapter unfolded when I witnessed Dad's passing. On January 3, 2022, Dad peacefully journeyed to heaven during his sleep, leaving an immense void in my heart. The person who cherished me deeply was gone, and tears flowed as sorrow gripped me. However, amid the grief, I found solace in the Lord's presence. Drawing strength from my faith, I resolved to carry on, honoring Dad's legacy of resilience.

At his memorial service, we chose a touching Chinese hymn, "The Lord Is Love," inspired by Psalm 23, to honor his life. On his tombstone, we engraved a profound message, "Love is patient, Love is kind," in Chinese and English. This verse came from Dad's other favorite Bible verse—1 Corinthians 13:4–8, "Love is patient, love is kind. It does not envy, it does not boast, it is not proud. It does not dishonor others, it is not self-seeking, it is not easily angered, it keeps no record of wrongs. Love does not delight in evil but rejoices with the truth. It always protects, always trusts, always hopes, always perseveres. Love never fails..." I found it remarkable how these words perfectly described my father's character. Throughout his life, he embodied the true meaning of love, practicing patience, kindness, humility, and gentleness, just as Jesus taught. While Dad never asked us to include this verse as his epitaph, we felt deep in our hearts that it would be a beautiful tribute to the extraordinary person he was. His legacy of love, empathy, and kindness left a permanent mark on everyone whose life he touched.

2 Timothy 4:7 in the Bible says, "I have fought the good fight, I have finished the race, I have kept the faith." Yes, Dad lived a full life and fulfilled his mission. He unloaded his earthly labors and enjoyed peace and beauty in heaven. During the grieving process after Dad's passing, I embarked on a soul-searching journey, reflecting on his incredible resilience and the deep connection he found with Jesus.

Then, I thought about my own life and could not help but recall the wise words I have heard countless times, "Be grateful." Even though I have gone through all challenges and struggles, I realized I have the blessings of good health, a loving family, supportive friends, and a fulfilling job. That's so much in life I should be thankful for. Though the pain of Dad's loss is profound, I feel comfort and strength from knowing that Dad is now at peace in heaven, enjoying the presence of God's love. One day, I will join him in heaven.

GUIDELINES

Practicing spirituality is a personal journey that can vary for each individual. There are many ways to improve spirituality:

- Cultivating mindfulness through meditation or prayer offers a profound avenue for spiritual nourishment. Even dedicating a brief five to ten minutes each day to meditation can lead us inward, granting us moments of tranquility, happiness, resilience, and insight. Prayer serves as an equally potent means to address our spiritual yearnings and freely express ourselves.

- Engaging in activities that resonate with you and align with your spiritual interest, e.g., participating in religious gatherings, reading sacred texts, and attending ceremonies.

- Exploring knowledge and finding inspiration in an informal manner, such as delving into books and tuning into podcasts, can be incredibly rewarding. For individuals who have encountered religious trauma, engaging in structured religious activities might appear overwhelming. In such cases, it's reasonable for them to steer clear of religious contexts and maintain some distance. Similarly, some people might feel that traditional religious practices don't align with their way of life. In either scenario, opting for nonorganized activities that nurture spirituality and faith is a viable alternative.

- Engaging with nature can be immensely fulfilling. Whether it's hiking through scenic landscapes, tending to a garden, observing the intricacies of flowers and birds, or any other outdoor activity, it has the power to foster a profound connection. This connection often leads to a sense of awe and an enhanced appreciation for the inherent beauty of the natural world.

Humans are spiritual in nature, and we are always searching for meaning. Through spirituality, we find meaning, feel we are not alone, and gain power inside and around us. Some people find attending religious services and organized activities useful, and others find solitary time beneficial. Some people find reading scriptures useful, while others immerse themselves in nature. All of these are helpful to develop and maintain a healthy spirituality. We can find a way that is suitable for us to seek the meaning, power, and wisdom that are more significant and brilliant than ourselves. Getting in touch with these meanings, power, and wisdom empower us with the right mindset, recharged strength, and unlimited resources.

CHAPTER 9

PRINCIPLE 5: GROWTH

In the midst of change, we often discover
wings we never knew we had.

—EKATERINA WALTER

"Pick me, pick me!" Almost everyone in the classroom raised their little hands and shouted. It was the day I volunteered at my eldest daughter's second-grade classroom in 2007. Witnessing the students' boundless enthusiasm left me in awe. Regardless of whether they knew the answer, their faces shone with confidence and joy.

This spirited scene was a world away from my own upbringing. Silence characterized my early Chinese classrooms, where teachers were the sole voices. Our culture taught us not to make a scene or attract attention. You keep opinions secret and do not publicly share them.

As an immigrant, the prospect of seeking better opportunities in a foreign land might sound thrilling, even glamorous. Yet, reality paints a different picture—one marked by challenges.

You start from scratch—from learning a new language and adjusting to a new culture to acquiring a new mindset and finding a new community that accepts you.

One of the principles for building resilience is to adapt to the environment with a mind primed for growth.

FACTS ABOUT GROWTH

Being adaptable and willing to grow means embracing change, challenges, and new environments with a positive attitude that believes one can learn and improve through effort and learning. We do not need to be Superman to survive the daunting environment because no one is a Superman. Instead, we need to learn and improve to thrive.

As Leon C. Megginson, a professor of Management and Marketing at Louisiana State University at Baton Rouge, suggests, "It is not the most intelligent or strongest of the species that survives according to Darwin's Origin of Species, but rather the one that is able best to adapt and adjust to the changing environment in which it finds itself." (Megginson 1963, 4). The fact is that everyone faces new challenges one way or another and needs to adjust themselves to survive. Adaptability is about recognizing that life is dynamic and unexpected things happen. It is also about being willing to make adjustments to cope with unexpected changes.

Similar to Megginson's point, American country music singer and television host, Jimmy Dean, believes we need to adjust ourselves when facing changes and difficulties: "I can't change the direction of the wind, but I can adjust my sails to always reach my destination" (Kuehn 2023). In the context of an ever-changing environment, the key lies in recognizing what we can control, which is ourselves. It's all about the art of adaptation and adjustment. Embracing this perspective empowers us to navigate life's uncertainties with resilience and optimism.

Dean's quote also implies that even though we may not always be able to control our circumstances, we can always control our mindset and response to challenges. This mindset, known as a growth mindset, means you believe your talents and potential will grow.

The idea of a *growth mindset* has been popular ever since Dr. Carol Dweck published her book bearing the very same title. Dweck explains that people with a fixed mindset believe their abilities and intelligence are static and unchangeable. They tend to avoid challenges, fear failure, and feel discouraged when facing obstacles. On the other hand, those with a growth mindset believe they can develop their abilities through determination, effort, and learning. They embrace challenges and consider failures as learning opportunities, so they become resilient in the face of setbacks. Dweck encourages readers to shift their perspective from a fixed mindset to a growth mindset, unlocking their full potential and achieving greater success in life. People with a growth mindset do more by working hard, exploring opportunities, and taking risks. They achieve more than individuals with a fixed mindset who tend to think their learning abilities fall within certain limits.

As mentioned in the chapter on my mother, she embarked on an incredible journey at a top research institute in Sweden in

1982. At forty-four, it was the first time she had ventured into a foreign country. Her growth mindset was obvious in her determination to thrive in her new environment achieving innovation in the field of duplex steel, despite her self-taught English. When I came to the US at twenty-four, I already found the experience awkward and hard even with twelve years of English under my belt—so I cannot imagine how challenging it must have been for her.

With a growth mindset, people believe in their ability, so they explore more and are not afraid of changes and challenges. Immigrants often have a growth mindset to navigate unfamiliar environments and systems, according to the *Harvard Business Review*: indeed, the "growth mindset" is closely related to that of an "immigrant mindset." People who are willing to uproot their lives in search of something better are the types of people determined to make change happen themselves. To migrate to a new country also requires a high level of confidence in one's ability to change and a high level of tolerance for uncertainty. More importantly, they believe in their ability to figure things out and adapt once they get there (Kelly 2018).

In life, setbacks can often lead us to blame ourselves or others, leaving us feeling overwhelmed and powerless to overcome them. But it is essential to recognize that these limitations are a result of our fixed beliefs and mindset. The key lies in shifting our perspective to cultivate resilience. As Anne Gradey, a keynote speaker and author, points out, "A growth mindset nurtures a passion for learning rather than a hunger for approval and changes the way we navigate challenges and adversity. People who operate with a growth mindset are more agile, adaptable, and resilient because they use fear as fuel, adversity as a catalyst, and growth as the true measure of success" (Gradey 2023). By nurturing a growth mindset, we can break free from the constraints of negative thoughts and talk inside of us. It enables us to unlock our full potential by learning, evolving, and bouncing back stronger from any setback.

MINDSET

One of my favorite TEDx Talks on the growth mindset is "What I Learned from 100 Days of Rejection," given by Jia Jiang (Jiang 2016).

Jia, an entrepreneur, was rejected for an investment opportunity when he was thirty. After reading a book by a Canadian psychology professor recommending readers to experiment with thirty days of rejection, he decided to extend it to one hundred days and record himself with the purpose of learning to cope with rejections. Then, he blogged about his experiences on a daily basis.

On day one, he walked to the security man downstairs and asked him to lend him one hundred dollars. The man said, "No," and then, "Why?" Jia turned back and ran away as if trying to escape his shame. He was sweating with embarrassment. He watched his recording during the evening, feeling funny but relieved.

On day two, he went to a fast-food restaurant asking for a burger refill and explained it was similar to a drink refill. The restaurant worker said "no" and mentioned he would check with his manager. Jia did not feel as bad as on the first day.

On day three, he went to a Krispy Kreme donut shop asking for Olympic rings-shaped donuts. He expected them to say "no." But the employee took ten minutes to design the donuts in such a fashion. It was the first time he did not receive a rejection. What a victory! The blog with the photo of the Olympic rings-shaped donuts went viral online, receiving over one million likes.

Jia got encouraged and continued his experiment, including working as a Starbucks greeter for free, planting a flowerpot in a stranger's backyard, and even teaching at the University of Texas at Austin. He was able to successfully convince the manager, stranger, and professor to allow him to do what he planned to do. Later on, he became a speaker and the owner of Rejection Therapy, a website that provides inspiration, knowledge, and products for people to overcome their fear of rejection. Through his experience, he wants to teach people and organizations to become fearless through his rejection training program.

The moral of the story is that it's important to recognize that rejections, setbacks, and failures should not limit our belief in ourselves. When we fall into the trap of a fixed mindset, we start believing we will fail and be unable to change our circumstances. But the story of Jia demonstrates the power of shifting our mindset and embracing a growth perspective. Launching a transformative one-hundred-day experiment, he determined to break free from the limitations imposed by his own beliefs. With each rejection, he bravely confronted his fears and discovered he could persevere and overcome challenges. Through this process, he realized fear was merely a feeling inside him and not something to govern him. Jia's story serves as a powerful reminder that setbacks and failures are opportunities for growth and self-discovery. By embracing a growth mindset, we can overcome the limitations we place on ourselves and tap into our innate ability to learn and adapt. It's a testimony to the resilience of the human spirit and the transformative power of believing in our own potential.

Storytelling and shifting views can be a powerful tool to cultivate a growth mindset. I realized this from the TEDx Talk, "How the Story Transforms the Teller," by Donald Davis (Davis 2014).

In a story about his father, Joe, Davis begins by telling his audience that Joe accidentally chopped his knee when he was trying to help the family at the age of five. Despite the medical interventions, he wound up crippled and could not do anything requiring hard labor. Using his own words, "I became one of the girls," feeling ashamed of being relegated to spinning flax and knitting socks.

From that time, his mother started asking Joe to tell his story again and again. He, being young and crippled, did not want to tell the story, believing that telling it would not change anything that happened. His mother told him that it was true, but telling the story would change *him*. So, she asked him to retell the story many times, especially focusing on what he would learn from it.

One day, his mother asked him, "Joe, today tell the story, and tell what you get to do now that your brothers don't get to do." All of a sudden, he was smiling because he realized he could stay in the house and read while they worked on the farm.

He began to think chopping his leg was the best thing he'd ever done in his life, and his mother was right that retelling the story did not change what happened but changed his view and mindset about the incident.

Because Joe could not engage in any physical work, he had to find alternative means to make a living. After high school, he attended King's Business College, which taught him numerous skills. However, the money he saved from selling socks and spinning flax was only enough for one term. He begged the college to allow him to stay and learn as much as he could until the money ran out. Within one term, he had learned business, bookkeeping, and typing, which the school normally taught over two years. After returning home, a wholesale grocery company hired him as a professional business manager. For the next twenty years, he raised five little brothers and sisters, a widowed mother, and an aunt who lived with them. Then, at the age of forty-one, he bought a small bank, started his career as a banker in town, and became a successful businessman in town. Everyone called him "Banker Joe."

Whenever someone taunted him as "crippled Joe," he did not become angry. Joe no longer lingered on his early tragedy but moved forward with a positive attitude. He realized his story changed from a suffering victim to a winner enjoying life's rewards. Because of his disability, he could focus his energy on education. He learned he was not miserable and disabled but capable of embracing the changes, learning new skills, and adapting to the environment. Furthermore, as he acquired a great reputation, many requested his assistance when obtaining loans. In his new story, he became a hero because he learned to overcome obstacles in life and attain success. The shift allowed him to not only accept the impact of the accident and not let it define his fate but also to treat the disability as a learning opportunity to succeed in other areas—business and banking.

MY FRIENDS' STORIES

Similar to Jia's experience, many of my immigrant friends faced setbacks, rejections, and failures, and it is truly inspiring to see how many of them emerged stronger and more resilient. To secure stable jobs and obtain permanent residency in the US, many of them made the courageous decision to switch their professions to high-demand fields such as computer science, quantitative analysis, and accounting. This willingness to adapt to a foreign environment demonstrates their determination and growth mindset. Not only do these changes benefit individual immigrants by opening new opportunities, but they also have a positive impact on places like Silicon Valley. These skilled and talented newcomers contribute their expertise to the rise of the high-tech industry and fuel innovation in the region. For instance, AsAmNews reports, "Immigrants make up 69 percent of the Silicon Valley workforce in highly technical occupations, including 26 percent from India and 14 percent from China. Other countries such as the Philippines, Vietnam, Pakistan, and other countries make up 29 percent." These immigrants are important contributors to Silicon Valley's economy (Yip 2019).

The stories of these immigrants serve as an important reminder that resilience and willingness to learn and grow are powerful tools for navigating new challenges and overcoming obstacles in a new and foreign place.

JULIA'S STORY

My friend Julia has beautiful eyes that radiate calmness, perseverance, and optimism. Her journey began when she immigrated from India to the US during her twenties and decided to switch her studies from marketing to database programming because that was a field in high demand. The path to America was bumpy with visa rejections and job changes, but she persevered. Due to visa limitations, Julia could only work as a contractor in each company, changing jobs every eighteen months.

As an Indian-born professional, it usually takes ten or more years to get to the last step of the green card process (US Department of State 2022). From 2002, when she first came to the US, to 2012, when she finally got her green card, she spent ten years changing jobs, trying to maintain her legal status, and waiting for the priority date of her permanent residency. She said, "As a consultant, there are so many limitations (without the green card). You don't get a 401(k). You cannot save for retirement. You don't get full pay because your consulting firm takes a lot of money, and they give you a small piece of it. So, it's really hard financially, and you don't grow in your career."

Despite facing challenging circumstances, she displayed incredible strength and stamina, refusing to let them overshadow her growth or dampen her future. One remarkable quality on which she prides herself is her thirst for knowledge and ability to learn. She was never afraid of new technology and was willing to spend hours learning new analytical tools. Through these years, she expanded her knowledge of database management to quantitative analysis and risk management areas in the healthcare industry and financial services, becoming a highly skilled risk professional. From Cigna to Wells Fargo to Charles Schwab, she brought her A-game to every workplace, pouring her heart and soul into her work. Her efforts did not go unnoticed, as she earned recognition and appreciation from colleagues and managers.

Her story is a testament to the power of continuous learning, perseverance, and a growth mindset. She serves as an inspiration to all who strive to achieve excellence and build resilience over difficulties.

LAURA'S STORY

Laura has been a dear friend for over thirty years. Her kind eyes shine behind a pair of glasses that add a touch of authority to her appearance. Laura embarked on her own challenging journey after immigrating from China in the mid-1990s. With a bachelor's degree in STEM, she chose to pursue a master's degree in computer science upon arriving in the US, hoping to secure a stable job. However, she was laid off during the internet bubble in 2000. She then decided to embrace a new path—one that led her to the medical field. Determined to become a nurse, she started taking classes and working from the bottom up. She said, "Memorizing those long medical terms and pharmaceutical Latin words was undoubtedly a challenging one. I had to recite them countless times and study for hours every day till late at night…" She had to overcome the emotional struggles that came with witnessing blood, learning to administer injections with needles, and facing the reality of people passing away. Making such a radically different career switch is something I could not imagine doing myself.

Her efforts paid off when she became a registered nurse in 2007 while continuing to pursue more education credits. Driven by her dedication to both her family and personal growth, she made the thoughtful decision to take on night shifts. This choice not only allowed her to earn a higher income but also granted her the precious freedom to pick up her children from school and do chores for the family.

Fast forward to 2020, when COVID-19 threatened everyone globally. In the city where Laura worked, there was a shortage of healthcare workers. An increasing number of COVID-19 patients overwhelmed every hospital while a number of healthcare staff got infected or died of the virus. She tirelessly worked in the ICU, saving lives even during the shortage of personal protective equipment. Laura told me, "We had a serious shortage of N95 masks and other protective equipment. I was stressed out. What if I got the virus? What if I brought the virus back home? I had to be super cautious every day." Despite these life-death concerns, she continued to work through the pandemic, dedicating herself to serving patients and saving lives.

Even though Laura was over fifty, she did not let her age stop her from learning and growing. Her pursuit of knowledge and self-improvement led her to achieve a remarkable milestone—passing her Nurse Practitioner certification in December 2022 after years of continuous study. Her adaptability and growth mindset built her resilience, proving she was unstoppable.

TERESA'S STORY
Being adaptable is not just about adjusting to challenging environments; it's also about embracing curiosity and choosing

what aligns best with your interests and personal growth, even in environments with numerous possibilities.

My friend Teresa's story is a testimony of being open to new opportunities with a growth mindset. She immigrated to the US from China to pursue her PhD in biology in the late 1990s. After a year, Teresa's curiosity to explore the world outside academia led her toward a master's degree in business administration. Her passion for marketing soon blossomed, and she began her career in database marketing, which eventually evolved into her true passion—data analytics. She transitioned from a database marketing professional to becoming a leader in Artificial Intelligence / Machine Learning (AI/ML).

Speaking of her adaptability, she described the whole process as an exciting "trial and error" adventure where she fearlessly explored new avenues. She said, "Over time, my field changed from database marketing to marketing analytics; then called data science, and now AI/ML. You have to learn and adapt consistently. Combining my science training and business education, I am able to connect both worlds and stand out as a hybrid leader in this quantitative field." Her incredible journey has made her a trailblazer in her company and a respected leader in the data and analytics community.

Forcing yourself to adjust to a harsh environment is not the only meaning of being adaptable. It means that with curiosity, you choose what's the best to suit your interest and growth in any environment, even though it may require you to learn new skills and explore unfamiliar areas. Teresa successfully transitioned from a biology researcher to a data scientist and eventually a senior leader in the exciting AI field in her company. Her story drives home the immense possibilities that come with a growth mindset. Her growth mindset and relentless pursuit of knowledge and other soft skills have allowed her to reach new heights and become an outstanding leader in her field.

EUGINA'S STORY

At the beginning of the immigration journey, securing a job and obtaining permanent residency are top priorities for many immigrants. However, the journey does not end there because that is just the beginning of new opportunities to reach one's full potential. My friend Eugina's story is a perfect example of facing challenges and embracing changes for career advancement.

Eugina, a marketing executive at a telecommunications company, immigrated from Russia to Canada in her twenties and moved to the US in her thirties. Despite challenges as a non-engineer and non-native English speaker, she rose to prominence as a telecom executive. Facing rejection for promotions, she chose to practice self-love and confidence-building. She said, "I redirected my efforts, and I became more active in the Chief network. I wanted to grow myself. I would learn more about product management. I would learn more about female leadership…" She continued, "Just before my layoff, I achieved some key milestones for that goal. So that rejection gave me an opportunity to learn more—how to launch a particular product, and also how to become a better executive leader." Eugina was laid off in the summer of 2022. Once again, she refused to linger on the feeling of failure for too long. Instead, she continued to develop her leadership skills and expand her knowledge in marketing and branding. It did not take long for her remarkable determination to shine through, as she soon secured a new job as Chief Marketing Officer in a nonprofit telecom company.

With a heart full of compassion for her fellow immigrants, Eugina's desire to uplift others led her to write a book called *Unlimited*. Her remarkable adaptability and positive attitude determined her success in many areas and inspired many people around her.

AMY'S STORY

My friend Amy is another great example of adaptability and a growth mindset. As a senior consultant in the financial industry, her journey began when she immigrated from Vietnam as a refugee with her family at the age of six. Despite initial language and cultural challenges, she excelled academically and eventually received acceptance to a top public university.

Over the years, she has not only fiercely pursued personal growth and career advancement but has also taken on the responsibilities of supporting her own family and her husband's family, all of whom are new immigrants. As the first one in her family to complete a degree at a top US college, her education and fluency in English allowed her to provide substantial assistance to her two families, from playing the role of interpreter to supporting aging parents and in-laws while managing the family business. She faced numerous challenges while fulfilling her duties, but she showed immense strength and resilience with adaptability and a growth mindset. She said, "We all encounter obstacles. Challenging ourselves to step outside our comfort zone helps us grow. It's all part of the journey."

Always looking to embrace new opportunities, Amy's next goal is to help her husband open an upscale restaurant. While planning to keep her full-time corporate job, she tries her best to gain knowledge in other new areas, including web development, in addition to legal knowledge related to business operations and negotiations.

Embracing a lifelong learning mindset, Amy believes in continuously expanding her knowledge and skills in various areas. Her journey exemplifies the power of resilience, determination, and a passion for constant self-improvement.

SABINA'S STORY

My friend, Sabina, who immigrated from Argentina to the US in 2022, shared with me the incredible stories of her grandparents from nearly ninety years ago. Serving as a profound source of inspiration, their tales displayed the power of a solid growth mindset.

During the 1930s, a period marked by wars and poverty, one pair of her grandparents fled from Germany while the other fled from Ukraine. Hard work and determination contributed to their successful life in Argentina.

Arriving with no knowledge of Spanish, her grandparents from Germany ventured into this foreign land. Despite the odds, they showed remarkable resilience and became entrepreneurs, eventually establishing their own technology business. Similarly, her grandparents from Ukraine had no knowledge of Spanish. They only spoke Russian at the beginning and struggled to comprehend Spanish. Back then, the government assigned the new immigrants land to attract them to the country. Due to a lack of fluency, they worked for her grandfather's brother for free without realizing they were the owners of the land. By learning Spanish and through hard work, they eventually gained control of their land and transformed into prosperous farmers in Argentina.

Sabina is immensely proud of her family's values—resilience, adaptability, and teamwork. Now, as a technology executive, she finds herself following in her ancestors' footsteps—moving to a new country and beginning a new chapter in life. Compared to them, she believes she is in a better position because of transparent information and knowledge. She's much more prepared for the challenges than her ancestors. What has not changed are the family values she's carried on. A growth mindset and resilience inspire her to explore more options in the US. Her grandparents' remarkable journey serves as a beacon of inspiration, reinforcing the belief that with willpower and a growth mindset, anything is possible.

PERSONAL EXPERIENCES

I learned from my parents from a young age that difficult times sometimes are beneficial to us. "Difficult environments make strong people. You will always find solutions." Dad reminded me many times. In short, obstacles can create resilience. Mom repeatedly instilled in me that resilience arises from our willingness to learn and adapt to a challenging environment. "You will be able to learn new things no matter where you go. I believe in you."

In line with the words of nineteenth-century German philosopher Friedrich Nietzsche, "What doesn't kill you, makes you stronger" (Nietzsche 1889), I believe enduring challenging moments will only make us stronger. As an immigrant, from the moment I set foot on American soil, I knew I had to work harder and smarter to achieve my life goals. I embraced a firm belief that no skill, whether professional or personal, was beyond my reach. Challenges became opportunities, and I welcomed them wholeheartedly. Strength, for me, extended beyond the physical realm and into the mental one.

ENGLISH

Despite having lived in the US for twenty-nine years, I still grapple with the feeling that my grasp of English isn't as firm as I'd like it to be. Occasionally, my children playfully remark that my English skills are those of a ten-year-old. I mispronounce words all the time, e.g., *chaos*—which I once pronounced as *chows*. Subconsciously, I followed the pronunciation of Pinyin, the Chinese Roman alphabetic system. Whenever I order soup in a restaurant, I have to ask myself if it's *soup* or *soap*. Another confusing pair is *desert* and *dessert*, which I practice silently. This is the current me, twenty-nine years after living in this country and using English every day.

The beginning was much harder. I remember that once in a restaurant, the waiter asked me to choose "soup or salad?" I thought he said, "Super salad?"

I did not know what a super salad was, but I decided to try it. So, I nodded and replied, "Yes, super salad."

The waiter got confused and then asked me the same question again. I repeated, "Yes, super salad, please."

He had to pause and slowly asked me, "Ma'am, soup *or* salad?"

I finally understood him. Being embarrassed, I replied, "Any." I meant to say either soup or salad.

My friend had to chime in, suggesting I try the soup because hot soup would warm me up on a cold winter's night. I nodded, "Yes, soup, please."

I am still improving, and I enjoy improving. The thought of authoring a book was once beyond my imagination due to my limited English proficiency. However, I believe in my learning ability, and through book writing, I can elevate my literacy skills to new heights.

TOASTMASTERS

From my own immigration experiences, I came to acquire a mindset shift from feeling like a hopeless victim to a winner. Often in my career, I yearned to raise my hand and share my innovative ideas, yet hesitated due to the fear of potential criticism stemming from miscommunication. I masked my excitement when tasked with an engaging project, suppressing my emotions.

In 2009, four years after joining WF, my failure in presentations pushed me to realize my shortcomings. I was not confident, and my communication skills hindered my career advancement. Despite putting in years of hard work, my career remained stagnant. I started searching for solutions and wished I could be more courageous than those seven-year-old children in the classroom. "Pick me, pick me!"

One day, I saw a flyer in the office for a Toastmasters club open house during lunchtime, with free pizza. Lured by the promise of pizza, I decided to attend. I distinctly remember the club president's speech about her struggles. She was a woman from India, and it was her tenth speech. She did not look at her paper; she was confident, even with an accent. I noticed how she nonchalantly continued to eat her pizza right after her speech... I thought to myself I would probably have choked.

Reality pushed me to adapt to the new environment of a different culture and language. I could either overcome the challenges or back off to stay in my comfort zone. That day opened a door for me to see the possibility, growth, and potential. I decided to embrace the challenges and continue to learn. I joined the Toastmasters and started a journey, an unforgettable journey, to become a better version of myself—to become more confident, compassionate, and competent.

Joining Toastmasters gave me the opportunity to improve my public speaking skills. I felt much more confident at work, sharing more ideas and suggestions during business meetings and project discussions. I started gaining recognition and earned four promotions at WF from 2012 to 2019. I became a vocal team member not only in my own line of business but also in the women's leadership community and the Asian American community.

Prior to this, I found myself enmeshed in a vicious cycle of invisibility. I convinced myself that speaking up was unnecessary—after all, I felt like a nobody, convinced my opinions held no weight. This notion led to a self-perpetuating cycle: speaking less made me less visible, which resulted in fewer inquiries about my ideas, eroding my self-confidence. It was a spiral of self-doubt. Breaking free from this cycle required conquering my fear. As I shed those fears, I harnessed my focus and thoughts, empowering me to communicate more confidently and effectively. This newfound ability propelled my growth and allowed me to tap into my true potential.

Despite my children's playful teasing about my English, their admiration for me was a well-kept secret. At one time, several years ago, I overheard my daughter telling her friend on the phone, "My mom's bilingual. She's also an area director of Toastmasters." It was a moment that warmed my heart. I wanted to let my children know the momentum of learning and improving remains strong in me even past the age of fifty.

The undeniable truth is that the unyielding desire to learn, improve, and maintain an adaptable mindset is the key to achieving success.

GUIDELINES
To nurture and maintain a growth mindset, I've discovered three strategies that prove remarkably effective.

FIRST, LEARN FROM OTHERS AND ASK FOR HELP.
Similar to Jia Jiang, I feared the hurt caused by rejection. Even if rejections make us unworthy, I have since learned that rejection does not mean I am not good enough or worth helping. Behind every "no" lies a variety of reasons. Some individuals may simply lack the answer to our queries, rendering them unable to provide help. In other cases, limitations on their part prevent them from offering assistance. Sometimes, the misunderstanding of the request is also at play. But that is nothing to be upset about. We should not allow others to control our feelings. Ultimately, rejection is a part of life that should not define us.

There are three types of asking. One is asking for information; the second is asking for help; and the third is negotiating.

- Asking for information helps us to acquire the necessary information so we may clarify and reach our goals.

- Asking for help connects us with other people so we are not alone in the journey of pursuing our dreams.

- Negotiating helps us to throw ideas in front of others and find common ground.

I used to be reluctant to open my mouth to ask questions. Shy and embarrassed, I thought asking for help implied vulnerability—and that only weak people did so. I also did not want to inconvenience others, which I viewed as self-centered and selfish.

I realized the power of asking after getting assistance from others. When I had the courage to ask for help by overcoming my shyness, I found resources to support me. Also, many people enjoy helping others. For example, when I ask for directions on the road, most people are kind enough to give me directions. They are also willing to help others because it feels rewarding. I came to understand that each of us has moments of needing assistance, and that's perfectly normal. Our vulnerability showcases our shared humanity, underscoring our interdependence as members of society. This realization contradicts the notion that seeking help is a sign of weakness, instead revealing it as an essential aspect of our journey together.

SECOND, SURROUND ONESELF WITH INSPIRING PEOPLE.

When life takes unexpected turns and our plans unravel, we can easily feel defeated. It's natural to waver in our determination and succumb to self-pity. In such moments, the support of our family and friends becomes paramount. Their encouragement becomes the lifeline we desperately need. Therefore, curating a circle of positive individuals is vital. These are the people who provide not only valuable advice but also steadfast emotional support. By surrounding ourselves with such sources of inspiration, we create a network that bolsters our resilience and reminds us we're never alone on this journey.

THIRD, TREAT REJECTION AND FAILURE AS A LEARNING EXPERIENCE.

In life, encountering rejections is a natural part of the journey. What truly matters is how we choose to respond to these rejections, as our reactions shape our outcomes. Embracing rejections as learning experiences becomes a pivotal aspect of this process.

Ultimately, those who possess the capacity to adapt to new surroundings and harbor a growth-oriented mindset have the potential to unlock their fullest capabilities. By doing so, they ensure that they keep adjusting the sails of their lives, navigating the ever-changing currents of existence with resilience and determination. This is the essence of cultivating resilience through personal strength and empowerment.

CHAPTER 10

PRINCIPLE 6: COMMUNITY AND CONNECTION

Alone we can do so little; together we can do so much.
—HELEN KELLER

"How many masks do you have?" I asked my friend on the phone.

"Two boxes, with fifty each box, so one hundred masks. But these are not N95." My friend answered hesitantly.

"That's okay. I'll pick them up now. Thanks!" I hung up the phone, feeling satisfied.

It was two weeks after the government announced the shelter-in-place order in March 2020. Hearing the news that Kaiser Permanente hospitals ran out of masks, my three friends and I sprang into action, rallying the support of our

Chinese community via WeChat groups. Over one thousand Chinese members in the Berkeley area responded in force, overwhelming the four coordinators of this compassionate endeavor. In just one weekend, our community came together to raise $16,000 cash and collect over 3,000 masks, including N95 masks and 450 handmade masks.

We did not stop there. Over the next two months, we continued our tireless efforts to procure donations. We collected and donated thousands of masks and personal protective equipment (PPE) to various organizations in need, including hospitals, police and fire departments, local shelters, etc. I heard that all Chinese communities across the San Francisco Bay Area organized similar donations (Ma 2020). We were glad to support those in need in our community. Later on, I heard Chinese American communities across the country stepped up to the pandemic relief at the early peak despite facing anti-Asian bias (*CBS News* 2020).

Rallying community support to fundraise thousands in donations and masks manifested the effectiveness and power of being connected. In times of crisis, we can join hands to make a positive difference.

One of the principles of building resilience is connecting with the supporting system and community. It is about leaning on one another and finding strength to go through difficult times.

FACTS ABOUT COMMUNITY AND CONNECTION
Having a connection means we have strong ties with family, friends, and the community that provide us with support and a sense of belonging and purpose.

In nature, animals live in groups to survive harsh weather, protect each other from predatory attacks, and raise offspring together. Even trees depend on each other—for example, redwoods. In the article "What Kind of Root System Do You Have?," Susan Williamson, a nurse and a John Maxwell Certified Coach, described the incredible root system of redwoods, where "beneath the surface of these humongous, tall, statuesque trees are roots like an army of men who have their arms interlocked, standing and supporting each other. They are preventing the adversaries of life from knocking each other down. They are also making sure there is plenty of nutrients for growth to continue" (Williamson 2023).

I've always been fascinated by the beauty of tall and strong redwood trees. Little did I know their secret to resilience lies in their relatively shallow roots. "How can such magnificent giants withstand fierce storms and powerful winds with shallow roots?" I wondered. The inspiring truth is that redwoods stand tall and firm not because of their individual strength alone but because of the power of togetherness. Their roots intertwine with one another, creating a powerful network of support and interconnectedness. The strength they gain from pulling together is many times greater than what any single tree can achieve on its own.

The support our family received after the Tangshan earthquake in 1976 exemplifies the power of community. Alongside our neighbors, we quickly moved into the temporary shelter they set up using wood sticks, bamboo sticks, and plastic tarps on the street. It was a collective effort, with everyone helping each other. We cooked, shared food, and slept together in the shelter, and the kids enjoyed hanging out with each other.

Later on, when my parents sent my brother and me to Shiji-azhuang, my great-aunt's family and their neighbors in the village warmly welcomed us. Our community resembled the mighty redwood trees, standing together strong and resilient.

Just like animals and trees, human beings have learned to rely on each other to survive in dangerous situations through evolutionary processes. As individuals, we are weak compared to other animals in the wild. We are not as fast and strong as lions or tigers, but even large and powerful creatures like lions live in large groups! We humans, too, depend on one another to navigate through life and thrive. We have learned not only to rely on others to protect us when attacked by predators but also to provide food and shelter when others are hungry and weak and nurture them when they are sick and wounded. The design of humans is to connect and attach to each other to thrive in life. Our biological design needs this connection as much as we need food. As Bryan Parkhurst and Keith Tarvin suggest in "On Being Social Beings" under *Oberlin Center for Convergence*, "Humans are social creatures. We live in families, we work in teams, we envision duty and purpose through religious fellowship, we negotiate through economic alliances and political coalitions, and our norms are shaped by our culture, itself an emergent property of group-living" (Parkhurst and Tarvin 2021).

When we face life's challenges, our support system not only offers us valuable resources and solutions but also serves as a constant reminder that we are not alone in our journey. Our friend's compassionate ear, caring comfort, and companion-ship may become like a soft refuge amid life's storms. As the American Psychological Association states in "Building your resilience," "Connecting with empathetic and understanding people can remind you that you're not alone in the midst of difficulties. Focus on finding trustworthy and compassionate individuals who validate your feelings, which will support the skill of resilience" (*American Psychological Association* 2020*).* As we share our vulnerabilities with kind-hearted people, they hold space for us with empathy and understanding. This deep level of connection gives us the emotional support we need and helps us release our stress.

However, we often find ourselves caught in the web of disconnection due to the rapid pace of life, combined with the obsession with social media and screens. In "Disconnected connection: loneliness in our modern era," Brian Hollett and Ari Levy suggest human physiology hasn't changed much in the past thousand years, but the way we interact as human beings has (Hollett and Levy 2020). Although modern digital technologies enable us to have instant connectivity with friends and colleagues at nearly anytime and from virtually anywhere, these same technologies can hinder us from engaging in quality communication with others. We have hundreds of *friends* on social media, but seemingly no one who will talk to us meaningfully about our lives. It also quoted a recent study conducted by health insurer Cigna, indicating that of 20,000 American adults surveyed, nearly half of participants struggle with loneliness (Cigna 2018).

In another insightful article titled "How Loneliness Affects Health," Katherine Peters, MD, PhD, FAAN, associate professor of neurology and neurosurgery at Duke University, sheds light on this matter: "Loneliness can change the neurochemistry of the brain, turning off the dopamine neurons, which trigger the reward response, and causing some degeneration in the brain when the reward response is not activated" (Colino 2020).

Drawing inspiration from the example of the redwood tree, if only one tree stands there with shallow roots, a gentle wind can easily threaten its stability. Humans are the same: we are not as strong as when we connect with others during difficult times. In a fast-paced and ever-changing world where technology provides convenience, we need to pause and reflect on the importance of striking a balance. It's important for us to cherish the connections that anchor us and cultivate the relationships that truly matter to us.

PERSONAL EXPERIENCES

There is a Chinese saying, "At home, one relies on parents and outside on friends." My parents learned from a young age they could not survive without the support of others. They put efforts into building new relations and strengthening old ones with family and friends. During times of scarce resources, a bowl of rice from a friend can save someone's life. Having a connection allows us to get the resources and emotional support when we feel vulnerable, allowing us to achieve more toward our goals and dreams.

During our early years, we lived in a close-knit community where our bond with neighbors was strong. Our apartment unit (i.e., a studio) featured a shared kitchen and restroom with another family, and this shared space created a deep friendship between our two households. One Sunday morning, when Mom was stepping out to buy food, our next-door neighbor poked her head out with a hint of hesitation, "Would it be possible to lend me one Yuan?"

Mom's voice was full of sincere regret. "I'm sorry. I only have one Yuan left for the month. I'm on my way to buy steamed buns for the kids."

Our neighbor got excited, "How about buying us two fried pancakes too? We've run out of money, and there's nothing to feed the kids. I will pay you back tomorrow when I receive my monthly salary."

Responding to the request, Mom brought pancakes, offering our neighbor timely aid she would recall with gratitude in the years to come.

When I was little, Mom used to take my brother and me to visit her aunt in Beijing, her only close relative there. Those visits were truly special, and my great-aunt always cherished our company. She would treat us to delicious fried crisp bread, yogurt, hawthorn cake, and ear-shaped twists with sugar. Even when money was tight, especially toward the end of the month, my mom would borrow from my piggy bank, which was full of coins collected from recycling soy sauce bottles, just for bus fare. She never hesitated, as the connection with my great-aunt was precious to her. What could be better than spending time with loved ones?

Dad had the habit of writing letters and sending greeting cards. During the holiday seasons, he would spend days writing letters and cards to his friends, relatives, and colleagues. December was usually the busiest time as he usually spent the entire month writing correspondence. I used to tell him, "Who cares about your cards and letters? They'll read it and then throw it away." He replied, "I would care. I will never forget their kindness." So, he insisted on his writing—using his way of showing his appreciation.

In recent years, I reminded him, "Dad, nowadays, people use email or text messages to greet each other. Or e-cards." He got interested in the concept, so asked me to teach him how to send e-cards. Although he learned to send e-cards after a while, he resumed his old writing habit. When I asked him why, he said writing with a pen felt more expressive, while sending a real card and letter by mail showed sincere respect for the receiver. Moreover, his friends were not very tech-savvy and not fond of using email. I've come to agree with him that I feel more appreciated when I receive a real card in a friend's handwriting.

Mom usually helped him at his side, sometimes adding new names, reminding him to mention the relatives' children's names, or checking his list to make sure it covered all people they intended to write to. Both of them enjoyed the process. I learned later that writing a letter of gratitude enhances the happiness of both the writer and the receiver. Since showing gratitude to others helps improve overall physical and mental health, it's little wonder they were happy all the time.

NEW FRIENDS OPEN DOORS

Like many immigrants, I came to the US starting from scratch. Everything from food, clothes, and housing to climate, language, and culture was new. With my old support system gone, I now had to forge new relationships. I did not know how to ask for help, who would be willing to help, or whether I could trust strangers at such an early stage. I was lucky to get to know Beth, my first American friend. I got to know her through my internship at the nonprofit organization where she was working as the office manager. "Lucy, you are smart. You are successful. You will be more successful." That's what she told me before I went to UCLA for graduate school. I'm grateful for having Beth as a dear friend who believed in me all those years. Because of her unwavering belief, I saw my potential, while her faith in me inspired me to believe in my ability and ignited a fire within my heart.

As I continued my ascent up the corporate ladder and sought the backing of managers, colleagues, and mentors, the significance of networking became ever more apparent. Over the past twenty-nine years, I have embraced seven roles in the US, including temporary positions. Remarkably, friends secured four out of these seven positions through referrals.

OLD FRIENDS ARE LIKE GOLD

Besides making new friends, I treasure my relationships with old friends who understand my past, lend me a helping hand, and offer support. The bond forged through shared experiences and memories stood the test of time and holds a special place in our hearts.

"Would you please show me how to make payments using WeChat?" I asked my friend, Yuan, with a hint of eagerness. It was 2017 when I visited Beijing after five years. Over the decades, my visits to China were several years apart, each unveiling remarkable changes in my hometown. Every return showcased the sweeping transformations—from food, clothing, transportation, infrastructure, and architecture to services, technology, and cultural shifts. This time was no different. The endless array of beautiful new products offered in the malls, TV, and commercial advertisements often dazzled me. Yet, the standout surprise was the technological leap. I never knew we could use WeChat, one of the premier mobile payment systems in China, which enables us to pay bills online or in-store and make peer-to-peer transfers. The days of carrying wallets seemed to have faded into history.

"Sure, let me show you," Yuan replied with a smile. Just like thirty years ago, when we were studying for the chemical engineering final exam, she spent the whole evening showing me the features step by step.

Yuan is among my cherished circle of seven best friends from our college days. In China, we did not have the choice of choosing roommates, and eight of us had the same dorm assignment throughout our college years. This chance arrangement evolved into a steadfast and enduring bond, demonstrating the power of true friendship. It is in these long-standing friendships we find comfort, understanding, and a deep sense of connection. In fact, we've playfully mused about cohabiting during our retirement years.

Despite residing in different corners of North America and China, we sustain our connections through WeChat or heartfelt phone calls. Whenever I find myself in their cities, I make it a point to share moments together. Their company rejuvenates my spirit, invoking the nostalgia of youth. I always ask for help and find various excuses and reasons to *bother* them. Wen, another dear friend from my cherished circle of seven best friends from our college days, extended a heartfelt invitation for me and my daughter to explore her hometown upon learning of my impending trip to Beijing in 2018. Touched by her warmth, I couldn't bring myself to decline. However, I had to admit my unfamiliarity with China's domestic flight ticketing system. Without a moment's hesitation, she purchased tickets for us online and generously shared the flight details. As she greeted us at the airport when the day arrived, a sense of comfort and affection enveloped my heart, reminding me of the depth of our bond.

Old friends are a constant reminder of who we once were and who we have become. Through the ups and downs of life, keeping a friendship with an old friend becomes an anchor, offering support, laughter, and a profound sense of belonging.

My friend Diane once shared, "Those who feel isolated face significantly tougher challenges compared to those with strong connections. I've witnessed this among my friends and family." While acknowledging the usefulness of social media and the internet as a connection tool, Diane noted a growing trend where people connect virtually yet lack substantial in-person interactions. She elaborated, "It's a barrage of quick text messages, Facebook posts, and Instagram scrolls, rather than genuine face-to-face conversations." Thankfully, Diane gets together with her two friends a few times a year for extended vacations and engages in hour-long phone conversations every week. She vividly recalled a trying period during her divorce and reflected, "I wish I had leaned more on friends and professionals for support." She wished she had asked for more help from friends and professionals.

One of the most challenging chapters of my life unfolded after my father's passing in January 2022. Amid the somberness, a heartwarming wave of condolences swept in. Friends reached out through messages, cards, and heartfelt letters, offering their support. Since it was still in the middle of the COVID-19 pandemic, organizing memorial services was not easy due to restrictions. In this trying time, a constellation of friends emerged as guiding stars. They rallied to create a blend of in-person and online services, simultaneously live-streamed. Each friend assumed a role—some managed refreshments, others organized equipment, and some orchestrated the program and reception. On the day of the memorial service, around one hundred friends joined us physically and virtually, bidding farewell to Dad. Among the array of floral tributes, two stood out, adorned with the label "Wells Fargo Friends." These gestures of remembrance and solidarity came from old companions at my former workplace, even though I had left the company two years prior. Their unwavering support and thoughtfulness resonated deeply within me, and a comforting warmth enveloped my heart.

GUIDELINES

How do we build connections and engage with our community and become less lonely? There are multiple approaches. I usually follow strategies to connect with others intentionally.

FIRST, ATTEND COMMUNITY EVENTS TO MAKE NEW FRIENDS

Intentionally making new friends is one way to start a relationship. It creates opportunities to show what kind of person we are and allows us to find new friends who match our personalities and interests.

A friend of mine used to struggle with shyness, and she recognized the need for change. Making a personal commitment, she vowed to proactively engage in conversation with three strangers at every event she attended. The initial attempt was awkward, yet she became more relaxed and confident with time and persistence. Within a span of three months, she managed to forge more friendships than she had in the preceding three years. Some of these connections even blossomed into close friendships.

Approaching a stranger at a party can indeed feel a bit awkward, especially when navigating potentially sensitive topics like politics, religion, or race. To break the ice comfortably, I've discovered the following questions to be safe and enjoyable:

- What's your favorite movie or book?

- What sport do you enjoy the most?

- What advice do you have for _____?
  (This topic should be neutral, such as buying a car, learning a new language, traveling to a new place, going on a cruise, hosting a party, mentoring youth, volunteering at a nonprofit, etc.)

Based on the other person's response, you can seamlessly transition into more questions or share thoughts related to their answers. This approach fosters engaging conversations that can spark lasting connections.

SECOND, GET INVOLVED IN VOLUNTEERING

Engaging in community service allows you to contribute to a greater cause and exposes you to a diverse group of individuals who share your commitment to making a positive impact. Volunteering can often lead to meaningful connections and friendships. I've found immense joy in involving my children in volunteering at places like food banks, senior centers, and homeless shelters, such as the Bay Area Rescue Mission. Through these experiences, I've contributed to meaningful causes and cultivated friendships with fellow parents who share the same compassionate values.

THIRD, JOIN A SOCIAL OR PROFESSIONAL NETWORK OR CLUB

An additional avenue for fostering connections is by becoming a part of a social or professional network. This offers the opportunity to link up with a broader community, broaden your social circle, and gain access to fresh resources.

As mentioned in the chapter on adaptability, I joined the Stagecoach Speakers San Francisco Financial District Toastmasters Club in May 2009. This experience not only allowed me to overcome my shortcomings in communication but also helped me expand my circle of friends. Everyone in the club was friendly and eager to help. Almost half of the members were non-native speakers—which gave me more security, comfort, and belonging. Based on the evaluation I received, I was able to sharpen my public speaking skills, gain confidence, and improve my leadership skills. In December 2015, I achieved the highest title in the Toastmasters program—the Distinguished Toastmasters Award (DTM). My club members' warm support definitely played a critical role in my accomplishment and building confidence.

Toastmasters gave me the perfect opportunity to jump out of my comfort zone. I not only served as the PTA president at my daughter's elementary school for two years but also took on Toastmasters club officers and various district officers' roles. Along my journey, my friends cheered me on, and I even won championships at area and division speech contests. Their unwavering support is inseparable from my success.

Another social network that brings me immense satisfaction is DragonMax, a coed dragon boat team comprising individuals from diverse age groups, backgrounds, and life experiences. This team not only provides weekly practices but also grants members the privilege of kayaking with the team's small fleets at their convenience.

Additionally, I take great pleasure in being a part of TG Taekwondo Studio. My journey here, spanning four years of practice, led to the achievement of my black belt. Beyond the martial arts growth, this studio gifted me with friendships that extend to fellow members and dedicated instructors.

During the COVID-19 pandemic, I felt isolated with remote work and longed for a connection with my colleagues and friends, just as in the day prior to the pandemic. With virtual meetings, spending quality time with others felt challenging. Besides the Toastmasters club, I joined Chief Network in 2020 and became one of the founding members of the San Francisco chapter. Chief is the only private membership network focused on connecting and supporting women executive leaders. I had the opportunity to grow acquainted with many women leaders and become inspired by their amazing stories and leadership skills.

FOURTH, MAINTAIN OLD FRIENDSHIPS

Nurturing old friendships is essential, requiring effort and connection. Rekindling these relationships can be a rewarding endeavor. Personally, I choose to reach out through phone calls as it allows for more intimate conversations. Through phone calls, we could catch up on the latest happenings and share moments of vulnerability, where we can openly seek assistance and support. After all, any relationship flourishes when cultivated with care.

FIFITH, UTILIZE ONLINE PLATFORMS

Nowadays, technology brings us closer to family, friends, and acquaintances as it easily puts us in touch with those we have not communicated with in a long time or in a remote place. For example, my family relies on Messenger or FaceTime for our weekly family calls. During the shelter-in-place period, connection became crucial as we adapted to working and studying from home. Platforms like Zoom and Google Meet became essential tools.

Online platforms can be a great way to initiate connections that may later transition into off-line interactions and prove especially beneficial to introverts. For people with disabilities, technology can be one of the few ways to connect with others. It offers a range of benefits, including access to information and resources, virtual support communities, remote accessibility, employment opportunities, and flexibility.

SIXTH, PRACTICE ACTIVE LISTENING

When interacting with others, we want to focus on being active listeners by showing interest in their experiences and feelings. We want to be present in conversations, ask open-ended questions, and show empathy. Authentic connections build on mutual understanding and open minds for exchanging ideas and emotions.

SEVENTH, DARE TO ASK FOR HELP AND SPEAK UP

Asking for help is a good way to connect with others. It is to invite others into our lives and become part of our life journey. This kind of asking can extend into negotiating, for instance, job offers, promotions, or involvement in new projects. As an immigrant, I did not know I could ask for a promotion, believing hard work and dedication were sufficient. I later realized asking for a promotion was better than waiting patiently for one since it showed I deserved a promotion and expressed my willingness to take on more challenging roles and responsibilities. Even a rejection can serve as an opportunity to obtain future promotions. Asking specific questions can help me understand where I am and how far I am heading.

Asking is art. You want to be sincere, specific, and curious. Also, you want to compromise and find common ground, which needs practice. As with any speaking skill, the more practice, the more confident you become. Amanda Palmer, the author of *The Art of Asking*, said in the book, "Asking for help with shame says: You have the power over me. Asking with condescension says: I have the power over you. But asking for help with gratitude says: 'We have the power to help each other'" (Palmer 2014).

As an Asian American, I have observed that the Asian community tends to be reluctant to seek professional help when facing mental health issues. An article "Mental Health Among Asian Americans" published by the American Psychological Association reported that while 18 percent of the general US population sought mental health services and resources, only 8.6 percent of Asian Americans did so. A related study found that white US citizens take advantage of mental health services at three times the rate of Asian Americans (Nishi 2012). Perhaps more than any other group, Asian Americans fear being stigmatized for having a psychological disorder. Shame and embarrassment force many to struggle in silence and never seek help. It is time to raise the awareness that we all need help from others, and seeking help from professionals is a way to show we are strong.

Asking for help includes hiring a specialist or expert in certain areas, e.g., life or career coach, college counselor, personal trainer, etc. It also includes situations when we feel stuck in life or feel desperate: there is no need to wait until we become deeply depressed or seriously ill.

Speaking up is important because it allows us to get in touch with our values. Speaking up allows us to build confidence and communication skills. It shows not only that we are brave enough to share our thoughts with others but that we are vulnerable too. It helps us to connect with others and build a community, one which, in turn, may provide us with resources during our struggles in life.

Humans are social creatures. Having a connection with others is part of our design. During difficult times, we cannot simply just tough it out. We often rely on other people's support to overcome challenges. Therefore, we need to build connections, network, and cultivate relationships. Social relationships online are not enough. Face-to-face communication fosters higher-quality interactions than online communication.

CHAPTER 11

PRINCIPLE 7: A SIMPLE LIFE

———

Simplicity is the ultimate sophistication.
—LEONARDO DA VINCI

"Nothing you see here existed when I was little," I shared with my six-year-old daughter, standing together in our kitchen. This conversation took place a few years back when my youngest was working on a school assignment, comparing what kids have now versus what their parents had during their childhood. I continued, listing the appliances around us, "No oven, no electric stove, no toaster, no blender, no dishwasher, no microwave, no refrigerator…"

Before I could finish, she eagerly interjected, "No refrigerator? How did you store food? What about ice cream?" Her eyes widened with curiosity. "I got it. Poor mom—the ice cream was not invented when you were little; the refrigerator was not invented either."

"Not that." I gave her a wry smile, "Ice cream was invented a long time ago. It's just *we* did not have it; I did not know there was such a thing until I was older. Old ladies on the street were the only ones who sold ice cream bars... We did not need to store food. We rarely had any leftovers." I answered, thinking how simple our life was back then, simple and pure. It feels so unreal—and yet, just like yesterday.

One of the principles of building resilience is living a simple life. It means embracing a lifestyle focused on the essentials, contentment with less, and prioritizing what matters the most.

FACTS ABOUT SIMPLICITY

There are two facets of a simple life. One involves letting go of excess or unnecessary belongings. The other involves valuing important experiences, relationships, and personal goals over societal pressures.

Living a simple life encourages a shift in perspective, valuing experiences over possessions, meaningful relationships over superficial connections, and personal well-being over constant busyness. It invites us to reconnect with nature, appreciate the small pleasures in life, and find fulfillment in moments of stillness and simplicity.

Living a simple life can contribute to building resilience by enhancing a mindset and lifestyle that supports adaptability, removes mental baggage, and cultivates emotional well-being. Imagine, when we carry heavy loads of *stuff*, it is hard for us to travel on a long and strenuous journey. This stuff distracts us from our focus and goals, adds burdens to our body and mind, and weakens us when we navigate the mountains and ravines of life.

Living simply involves decluttering our physical spaces, letting go of excessive material possessions that no longer serve us well, and embracing minimalism. Simplicity also encompasses limiting our commitments and obligations, allowing us to create more space for rest, reflection, and meaningful connections.

However, we live in a world full of abundant materials and new products, so we easily find ourselves trapped in the lifestyle of wanting more material goods and instant gratification. We cannot resist the overwhelming stream of advertising that floods TV, radio, and social media. We tend to purchase newer, fancier, prettier products after comparing them with others. Based on an article published by Reuters, "Most women own nineteen pairs of shoes—some secretly," a poll of 1,057 women by shopping magazine *ShopSmart* found the average woman owns nineteen pairs of shoes. On average, women purchase four new pairs of shoes per year (Goldsmith 2007).

Because we expect instant gratification, we tend to fill our empty stomachs with quickly processed food to fit our working schedules or busy lifestyles. Technology has indeed liberated us from spending too much time on house chores, such as washing clothes and dishes by hand. But not all advancement is beneficial to our bodies. An article published by *Market Place,* "Processed foods make up 70 percent of the US diet," reported that while technology has allowed more efficient production of food, it has pushed the production of processed food to the next level, and they have become 70 percent of what most of us eat in America (Ryssdal 2023).

Our life has become complicated and hard because of wanting too many possessions. We need to be aware of the negative impacts of this complicated and hard lifestyle, which poses risks to our bodies and stresses us out. The wisdom encapsulated in an anonymous quote, "Fill your life with experiences, not things. Have stories to tell, not stuff to show." It resonates deeply with me—experience gives people greater satisfaction than material goods. An article published by Cornell Chronicle observes, "Glee from buying objects wanes, while the joy of buying experiences keeps growing" and maintains that experiences are more satisfying than purchasing (Lowery 2010). Chasing after materialistic things is stressful and meaningless.

Another layer of complexity emerges from the distractions brought about by the internet and advanced technology. Usage of the internet, especially social media, drives us to devote too much time to it, and we become obsessed with posting and comparing ourselves with others. We have become isolated from our friends and family because of our attachment to the virtual world. *Psychology Today*'s article, "Technology Use, Loneliness, and Isolation," states that technology compulsion may lead us to loneliness and disconnection and impact our well-being (Tahmaseb-McConatha 2022).

In recent years, the term FOMO (fear of missing out) has been trendy. According to *Very Well Mind*, it refers to the feeling or perception that others are having more fun, living better lives, or experiencing better things than you are. It involves a deep sense of envy and affects self-esteem. It is all because of an obsession with social media postings and comparisons (Scott 2022).

Living a simple life allows us to connect deeply—with ourselves, with others, and with the world around us. It's about slowing down, being present, and cultivating meaningful relationships. Building healthy relationships is a very important aspect of living a simple life. A healthy relationship means you feel truly connected, appreciated, and supported, instead of competing, comparing, or acting under social pressure or seeking personal gain.

Living a simple life is also about connecting with our values on a deep level. Having a connection to values creates a foundation for building resilience. But, Hustle Culture, which seems popular in recent years, makes us lose touch with our core values. Olga Molina, Doctor of Social Work, defined Hustle Culture as when a workplace environment places an intense focus on productivity, ambition, and success, with little regard for rest, self-care, or any sense of work-life balance (Molina 2023). The overwhelming demands and busy schedules can disconnect us from what truly matters. As we chase material possessions and success, we may find ourselves losing sight of the deeper meaning and purpose in life. If we let money, job status, and titles define who we are, we fall into the trap of seeking validation, social status, and self-worth through superficial satisfaction, leading to a sense of vanity and emptiness.

In the Chapter "Cause Three: Disconnection from Meaningful Values" in the *Lost Connection* book, author Johann

Hari says, "For thousands of years, philosophers had been suggesting that if you overvalue money and possessions, or if you think about life mainly in terms of how to look to other people, you will be unhappy..."

It also says psychologists know there are two different ways you can motivate yourself to get out of bed in the morning. The name of the first is intrinsic motives. They are the things you do purely because you value them in and of themselves, not because of anything you get out of them. Extrinsic motives is the name of the second. They are the things you do not because you actually want to do them but because you'll get something in return—whether it's money, admiration, sex, or superior status. Hari points out that we need to achieve the right balance when pursuing the various rewards tied to our extrinsic and intrinsic goals to avoid the depression and anxiety that arises all too often from materialistic values. Disconnection from meaningful values can have a profound impact on an individual's mental, emotional, and social well-being (Hari 2018).

PERSONAL EXPERIENCES

I did not feel life was hard when I was little, even though we did not have much. That's because I had loving parents who gave me a supportive and caring environment. Another reason was that all our neighborhood families were in similar circumstances, which meant we all shared similar resources and lived a comparable lifestyle. We also had a close-knit community, fostering strong connections between neighbors where everyone knew each other. These supplemented the lack of material.

Mom would prepare simple food for each meal: rice or steamed buns, one vegetable dish such as tomatoes or cabbage, salt, and soy sauce. That's it. "Wow, how healthy!" you might think. Wrong! We were skinny and constantly hungry. Eggs were probably the only main protein we could obtain back then. We might have some pork once a week, and good quality meat was only available during festivals because of the ration card limitation. Mom used to cook one egg for me and another for my brother every morning, but she would not eat any eggs to save money. You may wonder, "Who wants eggs anyway?" But eggs were precious and delicious during that time.

Cooking started from scratch back then. If we wanted to make dumplings, we started by making the dough, which would become dumpling wrappers. It was a long and complex process requiring skills and patience. Cooking was just one aspect of the simple life. Washing clothes was difficult, too, since we did not have washing machines until the 1990s. In fact, I learned to hand wash my clothes when I was about six years old. We used a scrub board to wash clothes and then hung out our clothes to dry under the sun. We did not have cars either, so we walked or rode buses. Later on, I learned to ride a bike when I was eleven because a bike had become a luxurious household asset and biking was a new trend at the end of the 1970s.

I enjoyed our simple life when the food, though scarce, was fresh and organic. Steaming hot buns straight out of the pot was my absolute favorite—warm, soft, and delicious. It smelled like wheat when I put it close to my nose. Taking a careful bite, the taste of maltose lingered in my mouth, and the texture was soft as cotton. One bite would satisfy my whole body. Sun-dried clothes smelled fresh, clean, and warm. To this day, I keep the same habit during sunny summer days and enjoy the fresh smell of the clothes afterward.

At the same time, biking kept us active and physically fit. We did not have too many toys or gadgets to play with, so we spent plenty of time playing outside and feeling connected to nature and our friends. It was a life filled with laughter and contentment without a crazy schedule or too much distraction. This slow life allowed us to enjoy the time appreciating nature and each other.

Living a simple life means having just the essential living necessities without excessive material or spiritual distractions. It is a lifestyle focused on avoiding unnecessary clutter in terms of material possessions and unhealthy habits, parties, or relationships that may bring negative energy or superficial relationships.

Kids nowadays spend hours in front of the computer or iPhone or iPad every day, whereas we spent hours with our friends outside running, playing hide and seek, or playing on rocks or mud. We went to each other's home and called each other's parents "auntie" and "uncle." Those were precious times of connection and simple pleasures that filled our childhood memories.

There is a Chinese "Wu Yu Ze Gang," （无欲则刚） meaning, "One is unyielding when one has no excessive desire." The idiom highlights the importance of restraining oneself. People will remain upright and fearless if they can resist temptations and inducements, remain selfless, and be free of irrational desires. The teaching is in line with refraining from owning too many possessions and desires.

I am not suggesting we all need to go back to a life that lacked resources because it's impossible to go backward when society has advanced so much. But the problem is we have grown too accustomed to our convenient and comfortable lives. With a click, ice cubes come out of the refrigerator slot. With a button, packaged frozen food turns into a hot and flavored meal out of the microwave. With a push, we can make fruit juice within a few seconds out of the food processor. When logging into DoorDash or Uber Eats app and placing an order, a full meal can appear within minutes at the door. It's about instance, convenience, and comfort. What a fantastic life we are living now! However, it's important for us to reflect on the balance strike in this fast-paced world. By constantly pursuing the fastest, newest, and quickest, we might miss out on the joys of living in the present moment and appreciating the *slow* processes that life offers. We need to find a balance between embracing the convenience of modern life and taking moments to enjoy the small things that bring us contentment.

I used to own only four pairs of shoes—slippers, sandals, sneakers, and leather shoes each when I was studying at UCLA. I added more after I started my first professional job and then more over the years. Eventually, I owned more than twenty pairs of shoes. It's a hassle to store and maintain shoes, especially the expensive ones. I had to keep them clean, wipe them, shine them, etc. I'd rather spend my time hiking, biking, and rollerblading. I realized I did not need that many when we were packing to move from our apartment to a new house. After cleaning up, I still own sixteen pairs today but only wear four pairs of shoes regularly.

In the world of pursuing extrinsic goals—a larger house, a newer car, a higher salary, a more attractive title, we are so tied up with going after the next new thing or the next level of validation of self-worth. We keep posting pictures on social media to prove our happy life, with the purpose of proving our self-worth and identity. We constantly compare ourselves with others. We are jealous of others and want to make others jealous of us as well. We care too much about how many *likes* we receive on our social media posts. We eventually lose our focus on our intrinsic values while our internal light vanishes in the process.

I thought about my enlightening moment in 2021, the second year of the COVID-19 pandemic. "Go back to China! Go back to China!" My parents got yelled at on the street in Berkeley. They were shocked and intimidated. After living in the US for decades, they could not understand the reason behind the hatefulness. Was this still the same country embracing immigrants and welcoming newcomers? I was furious when I heard it from them.

Then, on March 17, 2021, I heard the news of the Atlanta shootings that shocked the entire nation. Among the eight who lost their lives, six were Asians. The chilling news sent shivers down my spine. As an Asian, particularly as a Chinese woman, I knew I could easily have been one of the victims. I began to feel vulnerable on the street during the evening. Even during the daylight, when I am the only Asian or woman in a room, even in a professional setting, I can still feel vulnerable. After all, how many will understand, stand by, and support me? I suddenly felt the need for an alliance.

The Atlanta shooting in 2021 was a turning point and a wake-up call for all of us. Therefore, there were waves of protests and rallies across the nation with the theme of Stop Asian Hate. In 2020, I joined the Albany Asian Pacific Islanders Parent Engagement Group (API-PEG) and initiated the Stop Asian Hate committee. The news of increasing crimes against Asians woke me up. If everyone minds their own business and does not speak up and take action, who else stands up for justice for us and protects us? If everyone's schedule is around their own busy life, how can we prioritize truly important matters?

Joining the API-PEG helped me raise my awareness of my own values and meanings. I believe everyone is created equal and should be treated equally. I want to stand up to support my fellow Asians and send a strong message: racism should be fought to the very end and diversity championed. I started to become active in the API-PEG community, taking on the role of the API Speakers Series cohost. I represented the API group to speak to Albany High School students in March 2022 as part of the Diversity and Inclusion panel. I was calm, confident, and articulate when I faced over one thousand students on the baseball field, telling them about my feelings as an Asian woman and advocating for Stop Asian Hate. I received many positive messages and greetings from the students afterward. Volunteering along with my Asian American peers allowed me to get in touch with my own values.

MY FRIENDS' STORIES

Among my immigrant friends, everyone cherished the values that motivated them to achieve their goals—love, hope, hard work, courage, growth, etc. Living a simple and focused life allows us to be in line with our purpose, value, and meaning.

GRACE'S STORY

My friend Grace, a senior finance executive for over twenty years, immigrated from the Caribbean to the US when she was in her twenties. Grace holds a thought-provoking perspective on American culture, one she believes compels us to prioritize spending on material possessions—a bigger car, a boat, a more advanced TV, and the like. She said, "At the end of the day, what is the meaning of all of that? What does it really give you? What really *does* give us happiness?" Grace raised a fundamental inquiry about our pursuit of abundance. Digging deeper, she continued, "We want to have some food to eat. We want to live in a decent house. But if we're continuing to aspire to MacMansions, why are we chasing after that? When I was growing up, I didn't have (much)."

Grace proudly identifies herself as an aspiring minimalist because she really wants to get rid of the extra stuff. In her opinion, "You don't have to have all those things. You don't have to have the latest and greatest. That's not important." She is raising her kids with the same mentality. When it comes to shopping for clothes, she takes a practical stance. Grace doesn't engage in elaborate shopping sprees for her daughter's wardrobe. Instead, when she notices her daughter has outgrown her clothing, she opts for simplicity—a visit to stores like Target or Old Navy, where she selects basic clothing items.

Also, she mentioned that lifestyle reflects priorities. Her family prioritized education and travel when she grew up rather than luxurious clothes and food, so she got the opportunity to see different parts of the world and became a foreign exchange student in the US. She appreciated her parents raising her with these values and believed it was important to teach children how to be more resilient and the value of delayed gratification.

YASMIN'S STORY

Yasmin, the friend I mentioned in a previous chapter who courageously cared for her mother during her battle with cancer, offers an insightful perspective rooted in her experiences growing up in the 1970s–1980s in the US. She believes people who have lived long and fulfilling lives didn't consume as much food or as often. She said, "In order to be in optimal health, you actually can't have too much rich food, meaning too much fat, too much protein, too much sugar. Without them, the body becomes more resilient." Building on this insight, she adds, "Medical studies about caloric restriction show that if they limit the amount of food they eat, people live healthier and longer—they look at those Blue Zone societies, like Okinawa and certain places in Greece." Blue Zones are areas of the world where people live a long and healthy life, up to and past one hundred years. One of the nine healthy principles of the Blue Zones is the practice of eating until you are 80 percent full (Buettner 2016).

Yasmin believed living a simple life in a tight-knit community contributes to a happy life. Drawing inspiration from the concept of Blue Zone societies, she maintains, "In small villages wherever people have not much food, they're happy because as long as they have enough to eat, they're content with that. Joy is derived from interactions with other people." For Yasmin, you cannot overstate the value of human connections. She recalls her childhood when fancy phones and gadgets were not a part of their lives, yet they had endless fun playing with each other. It made her realize true happiness doesn't require much as long as you meet basic needs like food.

MASTER MIN'S STORY

Let's look at my taekwondo master Master Min's story. He immigrated from Korea in his twenties and recalled his struggle when he graduated from college in the US. At that time, he could not secure a job that matched his major—arts and animation design—so he decided to open a taekwondo studio, TG Taekwondo, with a partner teaching kids to get his green card, even though he disliked kids and had no interest in children's education.

When his partner quit after six months, he suffered a panic attack. Realizing he could not run the studio without his partner, who had an instruction certification, he became depressed and wanted to shut down the studio. During his desperation, he slowed down, prayed, and got in touch with his true feelings and values. When it was quiet, he suddenly realized God is love. One phrase that came to him was, "Love the children." He had woken up and confirmed his life's meaning was to share love with others. What else could be more meaningful than loving the children? Chasing after material possessions, including job security, career advancement, or business success, was not fulfilling without love and passion for helping others.

He laughed and admitted to me, "I used to count money when I counted students in the studio... Instead of counting one kid, two kids, I used to count $100, $200." He continued, "I was a changed man after that realization—love the children. I started running my business based on the love of children. I sincerely love them, and I treat them as loving and precious children."

From that moment on, Master Min transformed his approach to running the taekwondo studio. Instead of merely focusing on financial gains, he started operating the business based on a deep love for the children he taught. Even though he continued to struggle for the first few years financially, he did not give up. He made TG Taekwondo successful eventually through hard work, determination, and passion. As time went on, Master Min expanded the taekwondo studio's offerings to include a learning center program for after-school care, an inter-high center for high school students, and college prep programs. These initiatives fostered academic development and provided emotional support and a safe environment for the youths involved. Through his loving and caring approach, Master Min has touched the lives of many children and teenagers. He said, "The students open up through the program and really feel the sense of community. They feel safe here, and that's the purpose. We offer love to the students."

Some students with learning disabilities improved significantly, while others who were struggling with various challenges found solace and a sense of belonging in the loving environment he created. Some students managed to overcome bad habits like lack of discipline, self-control, or drug reliance, making inspiring positive changes in their lives.

Master Min's dedication didn't stop there. He also offered internship and job opportunities to teenagers, helping them grow into responsible and confident individuals. He took his students on trips for competitions, volunteering, and community-building activities, encouraging their personal growth and development. Some students even excelled at the national level, becoming part of Team USA.

Now, he has become an accomplished entrepreneur after twenty years. Getting in touch with his true values and living with those values motivated Master Min to get up every morning to run his business passionately. His company has become a sought-after business and learning center in the area. His story is a powerful reminder of the impact that living with true values and pursuing a heartfelt purpose can bring not just financial success but also personal success in positively shaping the lives of others.

GUIDELINES

We need to live a simple life that is slow, focused, and clear. That is the key to having a healthy, relaxed, and joyful life. Living a simple life nurtures our body and soul, allowing us to focus on the most important things in our lives—health, relationships, and values. Through simplicity, we establish a foundation that empowers us to effectively manage stress and fortify our resilience in times of challenge. By simplifying our existence, we create space to thrive and cherish what truly matters.

To change our lifestyle to be simple, we need to consider four aspects.

FIRST OF ALL, WE WANT TO POSSESS A GOOD AMOUNT OF MATERIAL THINGS, BUT NOT TOO MUCH.

How much is enough? It's a hard question to answer. Each person has a different understanding of how much they need. While some derive happiness from material possessions, setting limits is essential. You may want to ask several questions before determining how much is too much.

- How much time do you spend chasing after the next new goods beyond essentials (meals and home)?

- How much money do you spend on these goods?

- How much genuine happiness do you gain from these goods?

In reality, our core needs are quite modest: three balanced meals a day, a comfortable home, and a handful of clothing and shoes. Our dwelling should radiate tranquility and charm. This home is a peaceful and lovely place. You should consider everything else excessive.

The following ways have helped me to assess and slim down my material belongings.

1. Set up a three-month schedule to assess closets and cupboards.

2. Remove the stuff that is not necessary or that we have not used or touched for a long time.

3. Donate, recycle, or dump.

Simplicity paves the way to a more fulfilling life by unburdening us from excess and allowing us to cherish what truly matters.

SECOND, WE WANT TO BUILD HEALTHY HABITS AND RELATIONSHIPS.

Healthy habits include eating a balanced diet, engaging in regular exercise, ensuring seven to eight hours of daily sleep, abstaining from smoking, and moderating alcohol intake. There are many online articles about eating a healthy diet. I have summarized several simple and practical methods for a healthier diet:

1. Shop a variety of vegetables and fruits.

2. Reduce processed meat.

3. Prioritize food making and be creative.

It's not easy to make a dramatic change in diet or any lifestyle. The key is to take tiny steps and make it a fun activity.

THIRD, WE WANT TO SET A LIMIT AND KNOW WHEN AND HOW TO SAY "NO" TO OUR KRYPTONITE.

Kryptonite is a fictional substance that weakens Superman. It resonates in our lives, too—our vulnerabilities. Kryptonite can present in any form, such as excessive food, clothes, shoes, makeup, or negative thoughts, relationships, or habits. To live a simple life, we need to remove kryptonite from our daily life. We need to tune in with our inner thoughts and voice so we may identify our kryptonite.

- **Say "no" to additives such as unhealthy substances.**
  Driven by instant gratification, we do not have the
  patience to allow our bodies to take time to heal when
  we are ill. A lot of us rely on pills heavily to treat discomfort or disease or lose weight. We need to trust our
  body to take time to restore and heal.

- **Say "no" to comparisons, including those via
  social media platforms.** The less comparison with
  others, the more relaxed our lives become and the
  simpler life we live. Our values do not rely on how
  many *likes* we receive under our messages posted on
  social media.

- **Say "no" to unwanted invitations.** If we say "yes" to
  any invitation, our energy will drain into those meetings, gatherings, or parties. We want to ask ourselves
  whether these invitations are in line with our values
  and whether these are beneficial or detrimental to our
  bodies and souls.

- **Say "no" to harmful or unhealthy relationships.**
  Similar to unwanted invitations, we need to ask
  ourselves whether this relationship brings us joy and
  peace or drags us down and makes us feel exhausted
  or unworthy.

The list of saying "no" could go on and on. The most important
thing starts with awareness. We need to spend solitude time
to tune in with our inner wisdom. Meditation or prayer is
a good way to get in touch with our inner wisdom. Several
questions we may ask ourselves.

1. Do I spend too much time or energy on this?

2. Is it healthy?

3. Is it making my life complicated or simple?

4. Is it important to me?

5. Is it time to say "no"?

Identify your kryptonite and take control. Here are some examples from my journey:

1. Too much sugar. My way of reducing the intake of sugar was to not buy foods with a high sugar content, e.g., cakes, cookies, and ice cream. I set up a rule: I will not eat these more than three times a week.

2. Social media. I became aware I spent too much time on social media such as WeChat, so I set up a screen time of one hour per day. Also, I reduced the amount of posting. It allowed me to spend more time cooking, cleaning, and writing.

Small habits can go a long way. You can conquer your kryptonite through small habits.

- Be patient with yourself.

- Find a program to join.

- Team up with another friend or family member.

- Hold yourself accountable.

With determination, you'll transform your life by eradicating your kryptonite through small, impactful habits.

FOURTH, WE NEED TO CREATE SPACE FOR WHAT TRULY MATTERS, ENABLING US TO PRIORITIZE OUR VALUES AND GOALS.

One way of allowing us to connect with our true selves is to have a quiet time and look inward, e.g., through meditation, solitude, or praying. Another way is to have honest discussions with a true friend. Or join a nonprofit organization that carries a mission in line with your values.

I would ask myself the following pivotal questions:

1. What are the top three values I treasure the most?

2. Who do I admire the most? And what characters do I admire the most?

3. What's my deepest commitment?

Through these processes, you'll uncover your true self, fostering a richer, more fulfilling life.

In conclusion, humans have innate strengths and weaknesses. Living a simple life may nurture our body and mind to keep us strong. Living a simple life helps us to remove distractions and focus on the most important things in life, such as healthy habits and relationships. We don't need to own too many things to make us happy and give us self-confidence. To live a simple life, awareness of our environment is crucial, along with curtailing our exposure to kryptonite. Initiating small changes to eliminate distractions and detrimental habits paves the way for a more balanced existence.

CONCLUSION

——

We have absolutely no control over what happens
to us in life, but what we have paramount control
over is how we respond to those events.
—VIKTOR FRANKL

Humans are incredibly resilient. Through millions of years of evolution, we have developed the knowledge and skills necessary to not only survive but also thrive in harsh environments. Our body and mind are built to endure hardships and possess innate strength and resources that allow us to bounce back from adversity. We might feel like victims of life sometimes, but we need to remind ourselves that we have the ability to control our attitude toward challenges and overcome them.

Throughout our lives, dark moments always make us feel hopeless and consumed by despair. These hardships and difficulties are inevitable. For my parents, these included traumatic experiences caused by wars, natural disasters, starvation, and political turmoil. For me, the challenges took the form of illness, early separation from my parents, obstacles in my career, difficulties caring for my aging parents, and raising cross-cultural children.

Nowadays, people face a wide range of stressors, including academic pressure, digital overload, financial burdens, uncertain future, social pressures, mental health and substance abuse challenges, environmental concerns, safety issues, and so on. Each person's experiences and circumstances may contribute to their unique set of worries and stresses.

I used to criticize myself often. For example, I beat myself up for not detecting my youngest daughter's illness earlier as I worried she could not recover from asthma. I lost sleep for many nights. Looking back, I wish I had known the coping mechanisms for my stress back then. For the following five years, her illness became the center of our family's focus and concern. However, despite suffering from asthma attacks every winter, she recovered completely after turning six. Through our care and her exercises, she has become more resilient, surpassing me in strength and height. I did not need to feel desperate back then.

Life is undoubtedly challenging, but it is through these challenges that we grow stronger and more resilient. I am not recommending you gain resilience through actively seeking out suffering. If you have a choice to avoid suffering and trauma, then it is always preferable to avoid unnecessary pain. By observing how my parents navigated and overcame difficulties in their lives, I gained insights, inspiration, and valuable lessons that helped me develop my own resilience. Therefore, you can build resilience by observing other people's life experiences.

Growing up in China, we learned to tough it out, never cry in front of others, work hard, and never complain. We have an idiom, "You've got to swallow your knocked-out teeth after getting punched in the face." A mental breakdown means you are too weak to handle difficulties, and you'd better learn to be strong and tough. One teacher used to tell us, "If you never experienced starvation, you never experienced hardship." In other words, "If you have enough food to eat, nothing is a big deal." It's the mentality we adopted growing up in the 1970s–1980s in China. The world has evolved to the point where material resources are abundant in many developed countries, and a lot of complicated situations might not be solved through toughness.

Building resilience needs to be based on enhancing our human body and mind, not just *toughing it out*. That's why the first principle is about nurturing and healing our body, and the last principle is about living a simple life. Both principles go hand in hand by following our body's needs and creating a nourishing environment for ourselves.

Based on my parents' stories and my personal experience, I've arrived at seven principles that help us to respond to life's difficulties by building resilience. These principles have timeless and universal values that can help you overcome your life challenges. You might feel stuck in life right now because of your circumstances. These seven principles are intertwined to support and amplify each other.

Principle 1: Nurturing and Healing: This principle stresses the importance of caring for ourselves and others by promoting healing and well-being and believing in our built-in strength.

Nurturing can cultivate stamina, encouraging us to practice self-care, and self-compassion toward ourselves and others.

Nurturing and healing also help restore our body and mind, enhancing our confidence through a healthy lifestyle. During difficult times, it helps us to cultivate resilience, restore energy, and create a positive mindset and environment.

At the same time, this principle establishes a solid foundation for keeping us hopeful and grateful, remaining adaptable, and connecting with others and God or a greater source.

Principle 2: Having Goals, Hopes, and Dreams: This principle encourages us to set meaningful goals, cultivate aspirations, and pursue our dreams to find fulfillment and purpose in life.

By reflecting on our passions and dreams, we can strive for personal fulfillment and purpose and not lose sight of meaningful goals. This not only provides direction and motivation but also strengthens our determination to put efforts into achieving what truly matters to us. The principle allows us to concentrate on a bright future which helps us to overcome present obstacles.

This principle not only provides us with the motivation to nurture, heal, and connect with others but also leads us to seek spirituality and adjust to adapt while keeping us grateful.

Principle 3: Being Grateful and Content: This principle highlights the significance of practicing gratitude and finding contentment in the present moment, appreciating what we have rather than focusing on what we lack.

Gratitude fosters positive psychology, increases our overall satisfaction, and focuses on our blessings. Contentment helps us to accept what we cannot control with a peaceful mind. Whether the condition we face is gratifying or frustrating, keeping a grateful and peaceful heart helps us to face challenges in life and find solutions to overcome hardships.

This principle allows us to accept anything fate throws at us, which gives us the power to nurture and heal, restore hope, connect with God or a greater source, adapt to challenging environments, and connect with others.

Principle 4: Spirituality and Faith: This principle affirms the role of spirituality and faith in providing meaning, guidance, and a sense of connection to something greater and more powerful than ourselves.

Spirituality provides a place to appreciate life's goodness, allows us to navigate challenges, empowers us with resources, and strengthens our minds.

This principle nurtures us, gives us hope and gratitude, and empowers us to be adaptable and connected with others.

Principle 5: Being Adaptable with a Growth Mind: This principle emphasizes the importance of having a growth mindset, being open to change, and embracing challenges as opportunities for personal and intellectual growth.

By maintaining a positive mindset and flexible attitude, we can learn from our failures, develop new skills, and be open to new ideas to adapt to the ever-changing circumstances of life. This principle helps us to believe in our abilities and seek solutions during difficult times.

This principle gives us flexibility, positivity, and hope while restoring our nurturing ability and gratitude and helping us to connect with others.

Principle 6: Being Connected: This principle emphasizes the value of fostering connections with others, building and maintaining relationships, and cultivating a sense of belonging and community.

Social connections contribute to our success and provide emotional support, offering opportunities for collaboration, learning, and personal growth. Connecting with our support system allows us to find resources to move forward toward our goals.

This principle instills flexibility, positivity, and hope; restores our nurturing ability and gratitude; and helps us to connect with others.

Principle 7: Living a Simple Life: This principle encourages simplifying our lives, reducing clutter, and focusing on the essential aspects that bring us joy and fulfillment, freeing ourselves from excessive materialism and complexity.

By simplifying our lifestyles, we can free up time, energy, and resources to engage in activities that align with our values and contribute to our well-being. Simplicity allows us to focus on the most important things in life and not get distracted by noise.

This principle helps us focus on essential connections and core values that align with our hope, spirituality, and faith. It allows us to live a healthy life that is nurturing and healing.

These seven principles are useful tools during stressful times. I made numerous mistakes and failed many times throughout my life. I lost important immigration documents, missed my DMV road test, failed my professional engineering exam twice, argued with my colleagues, yelled at my children, lost confidence in front of audiences on stage, and many more. There were countless times I allowed my inner critic to trample my heart and many sleepless nights when my own ego separated me from my hopes and dreams. I wish I had known these principles at that time.

Fortunately, I had no doubt about my learning ability and never stopped growing. Learning from mistakes and failures is part of human nature. I have gained valuable insights from unexpected events, including my own mistakes. However, understanding these seven principles does not mean I have arrived at my destination. I continue learning to apply these principles in my life because learning is a lifelong journey, and I am not a finished product. If you question your learning ability, it is crucial to realize you also possess unlimited potential.

It's important to note that while these principles can help manage stress, they are not magic keys to solving all mental health issues. We should view them as tools to assist in stress management rather than those that replace the guidance and support of medical professionals. These principles can empower individuals to tap into their inner strength and prevent themselves from falling into a mental collapse.

Additionally, they can also serve as tools for personal growth and discovering one's potential.

The seven principles have helped me develop resilience and enhanced my relationships with others, allowing me to assist and support them. These principles have played a significant role in my growth as a coach, enabling me to empathize with my coachees and view the world from their perspective. Through their struggles, I have gained a deeper understanding of humility. I am grateful for the trust they have placed in me, resulting in me becoming more humble and empathetic.

If you find yourself frustrated with the vulnerability of younger generations, particularly if you are a parent, I encourage you to guide them in cultivating resilience by embracing these seven principles. Instead of criticizing them, consider nurturing their growth. Patience is essential as they navigate their own journey of development.

As I apply these principles in my life, I have learned that it takes time to practice as any other skill or habit, for example, New Year's Resolution. In "19 Mind-Blowing New Year's Resolution Statistics" (2023), De Boer reports that most people quit their New Year's Resolution before the end of January, and only 9 percent successfully keep their New Year's resolutions (De Boer 2023). I want to tell you that failure is fine, and you should always try to pick yourself up and keep going. We don't need to wait for the next big day or January 1 to make New Year's resolutions. Every day is a new day, a new beginning, a fresh start.

It's understandable if not all these principles resonate with you or if you find some strategies less realistic than others.

That's perfectly fine. I would be happy if you could apply some of these principles in your own unique way.

It is your journey that you will explore. You are creative. I believe in you. With your resilience, you will be able to become a winner and live a more abundant life.

ACKNOWLEDGMENTS

With heartfelt gratitude, I begin by thanking my resilient parents, who have been a source of strength and inspiration. My father, a brilliant, kind, and elegant man, instilled in me a love for literacy and storytelling. His belief in my ability to craft captivating narratives, despite my engineering background, set me on this writing journey. His passing fueled my passion to share his and my mother's stories, tales of human resilience and empowerment.

To the Manuscripts team, Eric Koester, Shanna Heath, Kyra Ann Dawkins, and other instructors and staff, my sincere appreciation for opening my eyes to this new world and helping me believe in the power of my own story. To Kelley Wilson, my marketing specialist, and editors Zen Grabs and Frances Chiu, your guidance, wisdom, and patience have been invaluable in bringing my stories to life.

A special thanks go to Eugina Jordan, who encouraged me to write this book and paved the way for me to become a published author. Your support and insights have been a guiding light throughout this process.

To my beta readers, I am deeply grateful for the countless hours you dedicated to reading my draft and providing valuable feedback. Your input has made my book stronger and more impactful.

To my cherished family, my husband and daughters, Angela, Elizabeth, and Maggie, your unwavering love is a constant source of strength. To my brother John, sister-in-law Shuli, niece Jennifer, nephew Andy, and sister-in-law Min, your belief in me and your steadfast support have been invaluable pillars of encouragement.

To everyone who stood by me during the presale of my book, spanning from the youthful age of twenty to the seasoned wisdom of ninety-four, your incredible generosity and support have deeply moved me.

Aileen Goh	Andy Chen	Bryan Hayden
AJ Umandap	Angela Ding	Caroline Gould
Alan Marks	Angela Federigi	Cecilia Li
Ali Dorris	Angela Shen	Chang Su
Alice Chen	Angelina Yang	Changyi Zhao
Amanda Johnson	Angie Huang	Cheer Cao
Amy Cheng	Anjanette Hebert	Chen Chen
Amy Hall	Ann Cripps	Chiungchi Wang
Amy Lin	Annette Zou-Viola	Christine Chandler
Amy Louise Aasen	Aubrey Carrier	Christopher Roldan
Amy Zheng	Benjamin Chan	Chunye (Carrie) Lu
Andrew Bennett	Bobo Leong	Daisy Xin Li

Dalai Jin
Dale Benveniste
Dale Carson
Dale Taormino
Dana Gilland
Daniel Rosales
David Won
Debby Poon
Deborah Han
Dennis Huang
Dongni Huang
Edwine Alphonse
Elena Keung
Elizabeth Brawley
Ellen Ross
Emily Fong Mitchell
Emily Wang
Emmelyn Kim
Eric Koester
Erica Moore
Ester Rabinovici
Eugina Jordan
Eunice Kim
Fang Chen
Fang Dixon
Fatema Basrai

Gavin Harris
Ge Xia
Ghita Filali
Haishan Zheng
Haixia Yu
Haoyu Wang
Heidi Lorenzen
Hong Shen
Hong Zhou
Hongliang Yang
Hongxia Chen
Hua Yu
Hua Zhong
Huangming Wei
Hui Kong
Huiling Song
Huimin Li
Huynh Schmid
Ivy Shen
Jacqueline Leng
Jamie Fossen
Jean Brewster
Jennie Byrne
Jennifer Liang
Jennifer Chen
Jennifer K Chen
Jennifer Chiou

Jennifer McGlothern
Jenny (Jing) Liang
Jessie Lee
Jia Yang
Jia Hu
Jia Jia Ma
Jian Tong
Jian Huang
Jianying Liu
Jiayin Wei
Jie Dong
Jifei Jia
Jill Guindon-Nasir
Jing Yang
Joanne Walters
Joany Xue
Joy Powell
Julia Cai
Jun Li
Junping Gong
Karen Gee
Karen Truong
Karen Wang
Kathy Doan
Kathy Rai
Kevin Moss

L Tong

Lara Thornley Hall

Lauren Van Wazer

Laurie Li

Lei Tian

Lei Xu

Leila Knox

Leo Chung

Lexin Chen

Lijun wang

Lilian Sun

Lilly Ji

Lily Zhang

Lin Zhu

Linlin Guo

Lina Park

Linda Rossetti

Lindsay Hua

Lisa Guan

Lisa Nelson

Lisa Yang

Lixa Marie Anderson

Lizhen Zheng

Loren Rosario-Maldonado

Lu Jin

Lucie Newcomb

Lucy Wu

Lucy Xie

Lulu Wang

Lydia Guan

Lydia Zhang

Lynn Casey

Margaret Tang

Margaret Mays

Marion Parrish

May Shiu

May Adams

May Chan

May Yuan

Meghan Doscher

Mei Wang

Melanie Rothstein

Mengzhi Hu

Mibo Gong

Michele Ching

Michele Ling

Michele Nealon

Michelle Kong

Michelle Pecak

Michelle Bufano

Michelle Finocchi

Mike Nie

Milton Chak

Min Ding

Mindi Cheung

Misty Farr

Mochen Ding

Mona Tavss

Monica Bloom

Monica Chen

Monika Cechova

Na Luo

Nabil Jarachi

Nadia Boucherk

Nai Kanell

Nan Li

Nan Wang

Nancy Zhang

Natasha Durkins

Nicholas D'Souza

Nicole Arnold

Ning Li

Nyrka Riskin

Ofer Yitzhaki

Patricia Chadwick

Pok Chan

Qingyong Zheng

Qinglian Mao

Randi Lee

Rayleen Thielman
Raymond Ho
Regina del Barco
Regina Lau
Richard Wei
Robin Merle
Ruihong Xiao
Sabina Schneider
Sandra Lo
Sarah Montague
Serena Rao
Shannon Lum
Shao Song
Shari Begun
Sheena Yap Chan
Shelly Ouyang
Shelly Stang
Shen Li
Sherry Hsi
Sherry Linert
Shirley Chen-blum
Shuli Fan
Shuying Zhu
Simone W Johnson
Stephanie Falkenstein
Sujatha Asokan

Suping Shue
Susan Ji
Talila Millman
Taoming Gan
Teri Gooden
Tiffany Tsai
Timea Bara
Tom Srukhosit
Tracy Fong
Trish Burgess
Vermouth Li
Vernon Stewart
Veronica Flanagan
Vivian Wu
Wei Tao
Wei Wang
Wei Wu
Wei Zhang
Weina Wu
Wen Song
Wendy Collins
Wendy Hui
Wendy Wang
Wenying Yuan
Will Xu
Xiang Ding
Xiange Zheng

Xiao Jing Si
Xiaohui Chen
Xiaomei Song
Xiaowen Hu
Xiaoyu Zhang
Xinghong Zhang
Xue Ge
Yan Wu
Yan Jiao
Yan Wang
Yan Yang
Yang Huang
Yanming Xu
Yanwen Yu
Yao Li
Ye Han
Yi Lin
Yiling Yu
Youfang Liu
Yu Mei
Yuhong Wang-Brunner
Yukiko Brown
Yun Wang
Zhe Zhao
Zhongkun Liu
Zhou Yan Chen

This book is a labor of love, and it wouldn't have been possible without each and every one of you. From the depths of my heart, thank you for being part of this extraordinary journey.

APPENDIX

INTRODUCTION

American Psychological Association. 2022. "Resilience." *American Psychological Association.* May 2022.
https://www.apa.org/topics/resilience.

Brown, Clayton D. 2012. "China's Great Leap Forward." *Association for Asian Studies.* Volume 17:3 (Winter 2012).
https://www.asianstudies.org/publications/eaa/archives/chinas-great-leap-forward/.

IOM (Institute of Medicine) Committee on Palliative and End-of-Life Care for Children and Their Families. 2003. "Chapter 2 Patterns of Childhood Death in America." In When Children Die: Improving Palliative and End-of-Life Care for Children and Their Families, edited by M.J. Field and R.E. Behrman. Washington, DC: National Academies Press.
https://www.ncbi.nlm.nih.gov/books/NBK220806.

Global Talent. 2022. "The mental health of Gen Zs and millennials in the new world of work." *Deloitte.* May 2022.
https://www2.deloitte.com/content/dam/Deloitte/global/Documents/deloitte-2022-genz-millennial-mh-whitepaper.pdf.

Klein, Christopher. 2022. "China's Overlooked Role in World War II." *History.com.* May 18, 2022.
https://www.history.com/news/china-role-world-war-ii-allies.

McPhillips, Deidre. 2022. "90% of US adults say the United States is experiencing a mental health crisis, CNN/KFF poll finds." *CNN health.* October 5, 2022.
https://www.cnn.com/2022/10/05/health/cnn-kff-mental-health-poll-wellness/index.html.

O'Neill, Aaron. 2022. "Infant mortality in China 1950-2020." *Statista.* Jun 21, 2022.
https://www.statista.com/statistics/1042745/china-all-time-infant-mortality-rate/.

Prashad, Vijay, John Ross. 2021. "A history of China's fight against poverty." *Asia Times.* July 2, 2021.
https://asiatimes.com/2021/07/a-history-of-chinas-fight-against-poverty/.

CHAPTER 1: MY FATHER'S STORY

Benabdeljalil, Ilyas. 2023. "Why the Chinese Civil War was the Bloodiest in Modern History." *The Collector*. Jan 18, 2023.
https://www.thecollector.com/chinese-civil-war-bloodiest-in-modern-history/.

Mitter, Rana. "Liberation in China and the Pacific." *The National WWII Museum*. Accessed August 30, 2023.
https://www.nationalww2museum.org/war/articles/liberation-china-and-pacific#:~:text=Origins%20of%20the%20War%20in,war%20between%20China%20and%20Japan.

Smil, Vaclav. 1999. "China's great famine: 40 years later." *The National Library of Medicine*. Dec 18, 1999.
https://www.ncbi.nlm.nih.gov/pmc/articles/PMC1127087/.

TAO, LIQING, MARGARET BERCI and WAYNE HE. Accessed August 30, 2023. "Historical Background: Expansion of Public Education." *The New York Times*.
https://archive.nytimes.com/www.nytimes.com/ref/college/coll-china-education-001.html.

The Editors of *Encyclopaedia Britannica*. 2023. "Chinese Civil War." *Britannica*. Aug 17, 2023.
https://www.britannica.com/event/Chinese-Civil-War.

The Times Higher Education. "University of Science and Technology of China." *The Times Higher Education*. Accessed August 30, 2023.
https://www.timeshighereducation.com/world-university-rankings/university-science-and-technology-china.

Wingfield-Hayes, Rupert. 2015. "Witnessing Japan's surrender in China." *BBC News*. September 2, 2015.
https://www.bbc.com/news/magazine-34126445.

Witzke, Mark. 2017. "How Much of China did Japan Control at its Greatest Extent?" *Pacific Atrocities Education*. July 24, 2017.
https://www.pacificatrocities.org/blog/how-much-of-china-did-japan-control-at-its-greatest-extent.

CHAPTER 2: MY MOTHER'S STORY

Brown, Clayton D. 2012. "China's Great Leap Forward." *Association for Asian Studies*. Volume 17:3 (Winter 2012).
https://www.asianstudies.org/publications/eaa/archives/chinas-great-leap-forward/.

Du, Elaine. 2022. "Women Hold Up Half the Sky": A Woman's Role during the Cultural Revolution." *Union College, Spring 2022*. May 15, 2022.
https://muse.union.edu/aah194-sp22/2022/05/15/women-hold-up-half-the-sky-a-womans-role-during-the-cultural-revolution/.

Fredén, Lars Peter. 2015. "Sweden honors 65 years of diplomatic relations with China." *Global Times*. May 17, 2015.
https://www.globaltimes.cn/content/922076.shtml.

Kobayashi, Shigeo, Jia Baobo and Junya Sano. 1999. "'Three Reforms' in China: Progress and Outlook." *Japanese Research Institute.* September 1999. https://www.jri.co.jp/english/periodical/rim/1999/RIMe199904threereforms/.

Philips, Tom. 2016. "The Cultural Revolution: all you need to know about China's political convulsion." *The Guardian.* May 10, 2016. https://www.theguardian.com/world/2016/may/11/the-cultural-revolution-50-years-on-all-you-need-to-know-about-chinas-political-convulsion.

Yi, Xiaocuo. 2020. "Blood Lineage." *Made In China Journal.* March 6, 2020. https://madeinchinajournal.com/2020/03/06/blood-lineage/.

CHAPTER 3: MY CHILDHOOD AND IMMIGRATION STORIES

Connolly, Kate. 2010. "Angela Merkel reveals her East German food stockpiling habit." *The Guardian.* September 28, 2010. https://www.theguardian.com/world/2010/sep/28/angela-merkel-stockpiling-food-east-germany.

Rafferty, John P. 2023. "Tangshan earthquake of 1976." *Encyclopaedia Britannica.* July 21, 2023. https://www.britannica.com/event/Tangshan-earthquake-of-1976.

CHAPTER 5: PRINCIPLE 1: NURTURING AND HEALING

Ash, Alec. 2016. "Is China's gaokao the world's toughest school exam?" *The Guardian.* October 12, 2016. https://www.theguardian.com/world/2016/oct/12/gaokao-china-toughest-school-exam-in-world.

Brown, Brené. 2010. "The Power of Vulnerability." TEDxHouston. June 1, 2010. 20'49." https://www.youtube.com/watch?v=iCvmsMzlF70.

Frankl, Victor. 1984. *Man's Search for Meaning.* New York: *Washington Square Press.* P. 36. https://ia801809.us.archive.org/19/items/mans-search-for-meaning_202104/Man%27s%20Search%20For%20Meaning.pdf.

Harrington, Anne. 2008. *The Cure Within: A History of Mind-Body Medicine.*

Icahn School of Medicine at Mount Sinai. *Mind-body medicine.* Accessed August 30, 2023. https://www.mountsinai.org/health-library/treatment/mind-body-medicine.

Jockers, David. "Episode #185—Top 10 Strategies for Improving Deep Sleep." *DrJockers.com.* Accessed August 30, 2023. https://drjockers.com/episode-185-top-10-strategies-for-improving-deep-sleep/.

Mayo Clinic Staff. 2022. "Meditation: A simple, fast way to reduce stress." *Mayo Clinic.* April 29, 2022. https://www.mayoclinic.org/tests-procedures/meditation/in-depth/meditation/art-20045858.

McCullough, J.E.M., Liddle, Sinclair, Close, and Hughes. 2014. *Hindawi*. May 5, 2014. https://www.hindawi.com/journals/ecam/2014/502123/

Mckinty, Rebecca. "Rewire Your Brain with Mindfulness." *Neurotrition*. Accessed August 30, 2023. https://neurotrition.ca/blog/rewire-your-brain-mindfulness.

Pacific College of Health and Science. "Healthy Body, Healthy sole—Foot Health and Chinese Medicine." *Pacific College of Health and Science*. Accessed August 30, 2023. https://www.pacificcollege.edu/news/blog/2014/07/17/healthy-body-healthy-sole-foot-health-and-chinese-medicine.

Quinn, Daley, Sarah Bence. 2022. "Foot Reflexology Chart: How it Works, Potential Risks, and Benefits." *Healthline*. January 27, 2022. https://www.healthline.com/health/foot-reflexology-chart#what-it-is.

Rankin, Lissa. 2012. *"Is there scientific proof we can heal ourselves?"* TEDxAmericanRiviera. November 11, 2012. 18'51", https://www.youtube.com/watch?v=LWQfe__fNbs.

Reilly, David. 2017. "Human Healing Unlocked: transforming suffering into wellbeing." TEDxFindhornSalon. March 4, 2017. 27'25", https://www.youtube.com/watch?v=LUFgxkBPh4Y.

Wahbeh, Helané. "Spontaneous Remission Bibliography Project." *Institute of Noetic Sciences*. Accessed August 30, 2023. https://noetic.org/research/spontaneous-remission-bibliography-project/.

CHAPTER 6: PRINCIPLE 2: GOALS, HOPES, AND DREAMS

Backlund, Steve. "Viktor Frankl's Revelation of Hope." *Igniting Hope*. Accessed August 30, 2023. https://www.ignitinghope.com/viktor-frankl-s-revelation-on-hope.

Cañas-González, Beatriz, Alonso Fernández-Nistal, Juan M. Ramírez, and Vicente Martínez-Fernández. 2020. "Influence of Stress and Depression on the Immune System in Patients Evaluated in an Anti-aging Unit." *NIH National Library of Medicine*. August 4, 2020. https://www.ncbi.nlm.nih.gov/pmc/articles/PMC7417678/.

Elkins, Kimberly. "5 Ways to Keep Hopes and Dreams Alive." *Guideposts*. Accessed August 30, 2023. https://guideposts.org/positive-living/health-and-wellness/better-living/positive-thinking/5-ways-to-keep-hopes-and-dreams-alive/.

Frankl, Victor. 1946. *Man's Search for Meaning*. New York: Washington Square Press. Page 96–97. https://ia801809.us.archive.org/19/items/mans-search-for-meaning_202104/Man%27s%20Search%20For%20Meaning.pdf.

Ma, Moses. 2014. "On the Nature of Hope and Its Significance in Innovation." *Psychology Today*. February 11, 2014. https://www.psychologytoday.com/us/blog/the-tao-of-innovation/201402/on-the-nature-of-hope-and-its-significance-in-innovation.

Mind Tools Content Team. "Snyder's Hope Theory." *MindTools*. Accessed August 30, 2023. https://www.mindtools.com/aov3izj/snyders-hope-theory.

Raghunathan, Raj. 2012. "Familiarity Breeds Enjoyment—Why forced familiarity with novel experiences enhances enjoyment in life." *Psychology Today*. January 17, 2012. https://www.psychologytoday.com/us/blog/sapient-nature/201201/familiarity-breeds-enjoyment.

Tabas, Andre. "Asian American Rights Movement." Accessed August 30, 2023. https://asianamericanrightsmovement.weebly.com/.

CHAPTER 7: PRINCIPLE 3: GRATEFULNESS AND CONTENTMENT

Brown, Joshua and Joel Wong. 2017. "How Gratitude Changes You and Your Brain." *Greater Good Magazine*. June 6, 2017. https://greatergood.berkeley.edu/article/item/how_gratitude_changes_you_and_your_brain.

Chineseposters.net. "May Seven Cadre Schools (1968)." *Chineseposters.net*. Accessed August 30, 2023. https://chineseposters.net/themes/may-seven-cadre-schools.

Dickens, Charles. 1836. *Chapter 2 (A Christmas Dinner) of Sketches by Boz*. https://www.thecircumlocutionoffice.com/reflect-present-blessings/.

DiPaola, David. "Gratitude and Contentment Lead to Happiness, Health, and Success." *dceams.com*. Accessed August 30, 2023. https://www.dceams.com/gratitude-and-contentment-lead-to-happiness-health-and-success/.

Emmons, Robert. 2013. "How Gratitude Can Help You Through Hard Times." *Greater Good Magazine*. May 13, 2013. https://greatergood.berkeley.edu/article/item/how_gratitude_can_help_you_through_hard_times.

Harvard Medical School. 2021. "Giving Thanks Can Make You Happier." *Harvard Health Publishing*. August 14, 2021. https://www.health.harvard.edu/healthbeat/giving-thanks-can-make-you-happier.

Khorrami, Najma. 2020. "Are Empathy and Gratitude Linked to Each Other?" *Psychology Today*. October 5, 2020. https://www.psychologytoday.com/us/blog/comfort-gratitude/202010/are-empathy-and-gratitude-linked-each-other.

Koranteng-Pipim, Samuel. 2015. "Contentment and Gratitude." *drpipim.org*. November 2015. https://www.drpipim.org/index.php/467-contentmentandgratitude-1.

Millacci, Tiffany Sauber. 2017. "What is Gratitude and Why Is It So Important?" *PositivePsychology.com.* February 28, 2017. https://positivepsychology.com/gratitude-appreciation/.

Pearce, Jacqueline D. "What Is Contentment and Why Is It Essential For Happiness? 5 Benefits." *themindsjournal.com.* Accessed August 30, 2023. https://themindsjournal.com/contentment-acceptance-promotes-happiness/.

Talesnik, Dana. 2020. "Yale Professor Divulges Strategies for a Happy Life." *NIH Record,* Vol. LXXII, No. 6. March 20, 2020. *https://nihrecord.nih.gov/2020/03/20/yale-professor-divulges-strategies-happy-life.*

CHAPTER 8: PRINCIPLE 4: SPIRITUALITY AND FAITH

Bennett, Andrew. 2014. "The magic of words—what we speak is what we create." TEDxTowsonU. May 8, 2014. 19'12." https://www.youtube.com/watch?v=BVK4mWaS3F8.

Bright, Marcus. 2021. *"The Faith Factor: How Students Can Use Faith to Overcome Adversity." Diverse Issues in Higher Education.* Jun 29, 2021. *https://www.diverseeducation.com/opinion/article/15109553/the-faith-factor-how-students-can-use-faith-to-overcome-adversity.*

Hall, Eric. 2020. "The Covid-19 Pandemic Tests Everyone's Spiritual Well-being, Atheists and Believers Alike." *NBC News.* September 21, 2020. https://www.nbcnews.com/think/opinion/covid-19-pandemic-tests-everyone-s-spiritual-wellbeing-atheists-believers-ncna1240613.

Manning, Lydia. 2014. "Enduring as Lived Experience: Exploring the Essence of Spiritual Resilience for Women in Late Life." *NIH National Library of Medicine.* April 1, 2014. https://www.ncbi.nlm.nih.gov/pmc/articles/PMC3652895/.

Marx, Karl. 1844. "A Contribution to the Critique of Hegel's Philosophy of Right." February 1844. https://www.marxists.org/archive/marx/works/1843/critique-hpr/intro.htm.

Mathews, Andrea. 2021. "How Spirituality Affects Resilience." *Psychology Today.* March 12, 2021. https://www.psychologytoday.com/us/blog/traversing-the-inner-terrain/202103/how-spirituality-affects-resilience.

National Geographic. "Chinese Religions and Philosophies." *National Geographic.* Accessed August 30, 2023. https://education.nationalgeographic.org/resource/chinese-religions-and-philosophies/.

Scott, Elizabeth. 2023. "How Spirituality Can Benefit Your Health and Well-Being." Verywellmind.com. April 27, 2023. *https://www.verywellmind.com/how-spirituality-can-benefit-mental-and-physical-health-3144807.*

Sweeney, Chris. 2018. "Religious Upbringing Linked to Better Health and Well-being During Early Adulthood." *Harvard School of Public Health.* September 13, 2018. https://www.hsph.harvard.edu/news/press-releases/religious-upbringing-adult-health/.

Walsh, Kiri, Michael King, and Louise Jones. 2002. "Spiritual Beliefs May Affect Outcome of Bereavement: Prospective Study." *National Library of Medicine.* June 29, 2002. https://www.ncbi.nlm.nih.gov/pmc/articles/PMC116607/.

WebMD Editorial Contributors. 2021. "How Spirituality Affects Mental Health." *WebMD.* October 25, 2021. https://www.webmd.com/balance/how-spirituality-affects-mental-health#.

CHAPTER 9: PRINCIPLE 5: GROWTH

Davis, Donald. 2014. "How the story transforms the teller." *TEDxCharlottesville.* November 14, 2014. 17'33." https://www.youtube.com/watch?v=wgeh4xhSA2Q.

Gradey, Anne. "Shift Your Mindset to Build Resilience." *annegradygroup.com.* Accessed August 30, 2023. https://www.annegradygroup.com/shift-your-mindset-to-build-resilience/.

Jiang, Jia. 2016. "What I Learned from 100 Days of Rejection." TEDxMtHood. December 7, 2016. 15:23. https://www.ted.com/talks/jia_jiang_what_i_learned_from_100_days_of_rejection?language=en.

Kelly, Nataly. 2018. "Research Shows Immigrants Help Businesses Grow. Here's Why." *Harvard Business Review.* October 26, 2018. https://hbr.org/2018/10/research-shows-immigrants-help-businesses-grow-heres-why.

Kuehn, Kelly. 2023. "40 Quotes About Change That Will Make You Optimistic About the Future." *Reader's Digest.* Apr. 26, 2023. https://www.rd.com/list/quotes-about-change/.

Megginson, Leon C. 1963. "Lessons from Europe for American Business." *Southwestern Social Science Quarterly,* 44(1): 3–13. June 1963. https://www.jstor.org/stable/42866937.

Nietzsche, Friedrich. 1889. Twilight of the Idols. Introduction, xv. chrome-extension://efaidnbmnnnibpcajpcglclefindmkaj/ https://www.faculty.umb.edu/gary_zabel/Phil_100/Nietzsche_files/Friedrich-Nietzsche-Twilight-of-the-Idols-or-How-to-Philosophize-With-the-Hammer-Translated-by-Richard-Polt.pdf.

U.S. Department of State. 2022. Visa Bulletin for December 2022. *Travel.State.Gov.* https://travel.state.gov/content/travel/en/legal/visa-law0/visa-bulletin/2023/visa-bulletin-for-december-2022.html.

Yip, Randall. 2019. "Asian immigrants transforming Silicon Valley." *AsAmNews.* April 7, 2019. https://asamnews.com/2019/04/07/asian-immigrants-transforming-silicon-valley/.

CHAPTER 10: PRINCIPLE 6: COMMUNITY AND CONNECTION

American Psychological Association. 2020. "Building Your Resilience." *American Psychological Association.* February 1, 2020. https://www.apa.org/topics/resilience/building-your-resilience.

Cigna. 2018. "New Cigna Study Reveals Loneliness at Epidemic Levels in America." Cigna's U.S. Loneliness Index. *Cigna.* May 1, 2018. https://www.multivu.com/players/English/8294451-cigna-us-loneliness-survey/.

Colino, Stacey. 2020. "How Loneliness Affects Health." *Brain & Life.* October/ November 2020. https://www.brainandlife.org/articles/how-loneliness-affects-health.

CBS News. 2020. "Facing Anti-Asian Bias Amid Coronavirus Pandemic, Chinese American Community Helps Supply PPE To Front Line Workers." *CBS News.* April 17, 2020. https://www.cbsnews.com/newyork/news/coronavirus-chinese-american-community-donations/.

Hollett, Brian, Ari Levy. 2020. "Disconnected Connections: Loneliness in our Modern Era." *Shiftlife.com.* January 16, 2020. https://shiftlife.com/loneliness/.

Ma, Annie. 2020. "Rallying Community Support, Bay Area Chinese Americans Fundraise Millions In Donations And Masks." *The Silicon Valley Voice.* July 3, 2020. https://www.svvoice.com/rallying-community-support-bay-area-chinese-americans-fundraise-millions-in-donations-and-masks/.

Nishi, Koko. 2012. "Mental Health Among Asian-Americans." *American Psychological Association.* 2012. https://www.apa.org/pi/oema/resources/ethnicity-health/asian-american/article-mental-health.

Palmer, Amanda. 2014. *The Art of Asking. Grand Central Publishing.* November 11, 2014.

Parkhurst, Bryan, Keith Tarvin. 2021. "On Being Social Beings." *Oberlin Center for Convergence.* Fall 2021. https://www.oberlin.edu/oberlin-center-convergence/oberlin-center-convergence/learning-communities/on-being-social-beings.

Williamson, Susan. "What King of Root System Do You Have?" *johnmaxwellteam. com.* Accessed August 30, 2023. https://johnmaxwellteam.com/what-kind-of-root-system-do-you-have/.

CHAPTER 11: PRINCIPLE 7: A SIMPLE LIFE

Buettner, Dan. 2016. "Power 9." *BlueZones.com.* November 2016. https://www.bluezones.com/2016/11/power-9/.

Goldsmith, Belinda. 2007. "Most Women Own 19 Pairs of Shoes—some secretly." *Reuters.* September 10, 2007. https://www.reuters.com/article/us-shoes/most-women-own-19-pairs-of-shoes-some-secretly-idUSN0632859720070910.

Hari, Johann. 2018. *Lost Connection. Bloomsbury Publishing.* January 23, 2018. The chapter "Cause Three: Disconnection from Meaningful Values," page 93.

Lowery, George. 2010. "Glee From Buying Objects Wanes, While Joy of Buying Experiences Keeps Growing." *Cornell Chronicle. March 31, 2010.* https://news.cornell.edu/stories/2010/03/study-shows-experiences-are-better-possessions.

Molina, Olga. 2023. "Hustle Culture: The Toxic Impact on Mental Health." *talkspace. com.* February 20, 2023. https://www.talkspace.com/blog/hustle-culture/.

Ryssdal, Kai. 2013. "Processed Foods Make Up 70 Percent of the U.S. Diet." *Market Place.* March 12, 2013. https://www.marketplace.org/2013/03/12/processed-foods-make-70-percent-us-diet/.

Scott, Elizabeth. 2022. "How to Deal with FOMO in Your Life." *Very Well Mind.* November 16, 2022. https://www.verywellmind.com/how-to-cope-with-fomo-4174664.

Tahmaseb-McConatha, Jasmin. 2022. "Technology Use, Loneliness, and Isolation." *Psychology Today.* October 19, 2022. https://www.psychologytoday.com/us/blog/live-long-and-prosper/202210/technology-use-loneliness-and-isolation.

CONCLUSION

De Boer, Mick. 2023. "19 Mind-Blowing New Year's Resolution Statistics (2023)." *Inside Out Mastery.* Accessed August 30, 2023. https://insideoutmastery.com/new-years-resolution-statistics/.

Made in the USA
Las Vegas, NV
21 November 2024

12311641R00167